BEING

IN THE

SHADOW

BEING
IN THE
SHADOW

Stories of the First-Time Total Eclipse Experience

DR. KATE RUSSO

Being in the Shadow: Stories of the First-Time Total Eclipse Experience
First Edition, June 2017
Being in the Shadow
Belfast, Northern Ireland, UK

Editing: Shayla Eaton, CuriouserEditing.com
Cover Art: Carol Graham, CarolGraham.com
Publishing and Design Services: Melinda Martin, MelindaMartin.me

Sign up to Dr. Kate Russo's newsletter and connect with her at
www.beingintheshadow.com.
Facebook.com/Beingintheshadow
Twitter.com/DrKateRusso

Note: Terms such as *Moon, Sun,* and *Universe* are capitalized to indicate proper nouns.

Publisher's Cataloging-in-Publication Data
provided by Five Rainbows Cataloging Services

Names: Russo, Kate, 1972-
Title: Being in the shadow : stories of the first-time total eclipse experience / Dr. Kate Russo.
Description: Belfast : Being in the Shadow, 2017.
Identifiers: ISBN 978-1-9997078-0-4 (pbk.) | ISBN 978-1-9997078-1-1 (ebook)
Subjects: LCSH: Total solar eclipses. | Solar eclipses--Observations. | Solar eclipses--Popular works. | Sun--Observations. | BISAC: NATURE / Sky Observation. | TRAVEL / Special Interest / General.
Classification: LCC QB541 .R87 2017 (print) | LCC QB541 (ebook) | DDC 523.7/8--dc23.

*This book is dedicated to
everyone who participated
in my interviews of the
total solar eclipse of
Far North Queensland in 2012.*

Contents

PREFACE... 1

SECTION 1: AS ABOVE, SO BELOW 5
CHAPTER 1: Celestial Bodies: The Sun and Moon
(and a Shadow).. 7
CHAPTER 2: Earthly Beings in the Shadow................................ 13

SECTION 2: INTO THE PATH 29
CHAPTER 3: Totality Minus One................................. 31
CHAPTER 4: Eclipse Day 45

SECTION 3: READJUSTING TO THE LIGHT.............. 69
CHAPTER 5: Return to Normality................................ 71
CHAPTER 6: Eclipse Insights 83

SECTION 4: LOOKING BACK AT THE SHADOW 103
CHAPTER 7: What Can We Learn? 105
CHAPTER 8: Conclusion: Get into the Path 115

SECTION 5: ADDITIONAL INFORMATION............. 119
Official Eye Safety Guidance (AAS)............................. 121
List of Total Eclipses until 2030................................. 123
Previous Works 125
Get Involved! 129
Acknowledgments 131
About Dr. Kate Russo 133

Preface

*O*n a warm August morning in 1999, I joined a massive crowd of people gathered along the beachfront of a small French coastal village. I had waited fifteen years for this moment, and I was wide-eyed with anticipation.

I was about to see my first total solar eclipse.

I knew technically what was about to happen—the Moon would block all the light from the Sun, casting us into a dark shadow. But I was completely unprepared for the immersive experience. The temperature dropped, colors faded, the wind picked up, and the eeriness of the approaching Moon's shadow sent a chill down my spine. I held my breath as the world around me came to a standstill, and gasped as all remaining light disappeared.

I could not believe my eyes. A black hole appeared where the Sun should be. As my eyes adjusted to the darkness, I saw the corona—the outer atmosphere of the Sun—illuminate beyond the black shape of the Moon. It was the most awe-inspiring nature event I had ever seen. I felt how insignificant we are in our vast Universe. And for the first time, I understood that we are all connected as human beings through time and place. Lost in the moment, I drank it all in.

And then, just as suddenly, the Moon's shadow raced away, and light rapidly returned. Totality was over. I knew immediately that I wanted to see it again. I needed to see it again. I choked up, knowing my life would never be the same.

Almost a year later, I stood on a remote beach in Madagascar, waiting to see my second total eclipse. This time, the total eclipse was to occur in the late afternoon. Our small group of intrepid travelers and local tribesmen lined the remote beach, jumping up and down with excitement and terror as the Moon's shadow rushed toward us. Again, I broke out in goosebumps and shrieked unexpectedly as we were cast into the eerie darkness. Awestruck, I lost all sense of the real world as I stared wide-eyed at the eclipsed Sun. No picture or painting could ever capture the beauty and uniqueness of totality. There was no Sun or Moon—just blackness surrounded by living tendrils reaching out to nothingness. It was intense, beautiful, and emotional. This time, I glanced around me, and every direction revealed a magical new world. Vibrant orange and deep purple were visible all around the horizon, and the deep-dark-blue sky above was dotted with a few stars and planets. I screamed out as totality ended, signaling a return to the normal world. This eclipse seemed even more dramatic than the first, and I again felt desperate to see the next one.

We all marveled at the wonder of our Universe as the afternoon light returned. But nature had something else in store, as we sat on the sand watching the light dimming yet again as dusk turned to night. Watching that setting Sun made me realize the total eclipse was like a metaphor for life—beautiful, intense, and fleeting. As we camped on the beach under the stars that evening, I felt humbled, at one with the world, and incredibly lucky.

Seeing my second total eclipse confirmed what I knew from that very first total eclipse. I had an addiction, and I had it bad.

Since then, I have traveled to remote locations on most continents around the world to experience the total solar eclipse again and again. I am compelled to chase eclipses. It is something I must do, a part of who I am. At the time of writing, I have been chasing eclipses for eighteen years, and am *about to experience my eleventh total solar eclipse. I will be chasing eclipses for the rest of my life.*

As a psychologist, I believe the total eclipse is a peak human experience, and more than a moment of pure bliss. It is difficult to put the experience into words, and difficult to convey to others. The total eclipse is not just what we see, but it is also what we feel, how it changes us, and what we then become. It is a unique experience, and one I am researching to understand more about us as human beings.

In 2012, a total solar eclipse was visible across Far North Queensland in Australia, the region I grew up in, and where my family of origin still lives. As an eclipse chaser, this was an incredible coincidence. Instead of traveling to some remote region, all I had to do was go home.

I used the opportunity to stay for several months, engaging in eclipse research. I surveyed and interviewed over one hundred people about their eclipse expectations and experiences. I wanted to know: What did they expect the eclipse to be? What did they experience on that day? How did they make sense of it all? People loved sharing their stories. They wanted to keep the memory of the eclipse alive. I published many of these shorter stories in my second book, Totality: The Total Solar Eclipse of 2012 in Far North Queensland. The more vivid and detailed stories, capturing moments before and after the total eclipse, are included here.

This book is the story of the total eclipse told from the perspective of six ordinary people seeing their first total eclipse in 2012. They are not scientists, academics, or astrophysicists. These are ordinary human beings, like you, who were in the right place at the right time to see their first total solar eclipse.

As you will discover, the total eclipse is not just a scientific or celestial event. It is an awe-inspiring, immersive natural wonder of interest to every human being. Totality allows us to appreciate our world, while also understanding ourselves. I urge everyone to experience a total solar eclipse—it really is worth the hype.

Dr. Kate Russo

1

AS ABOVE, SO BELOW

CHAPTER 1

CELESTIAL BODIES: THE SUN AND MOON (AND A SHADOW)

Is seeing a total solar eclipse on your bucket list? Many people assume that a total solar eclipse is an event only of interest to astronomers. News stories about a total eclipse usually feature a bearded man with a telescope, talking flatly about how totality is meant to be exciting. Surely it can't be that exciting, right? After all, over-hyped events often turn out to be nothing like what we expected or are led to believe.

Many astronomical events need telescopes or binoculars to view. A total solar eclipse is an exception. It is obviously dramatic as it changes the environment around us. You do not need an understanding of physics or science to appreciate a total solar eclipse. It is a deeply engaging experience—things change and happen above you, around you, and within you. Many people find it difficult to put the experience into words, as it affects them so deeply. You don't *see* a total eclipse—you *experience* it.

You may not realize it, but your first total solar eclipse may end up being a momentous milestone event in your life, like coming-of-age, graduation, or getting married. It is *that* good. A total eclipse is an event you should experience at least once in your life. For some, like me, once is not enough.

The focus of this book is on personal stories of the total eclipse experience. But before we meet our beings in the shadow and delve into their experiences, it is useful to understand eclipse basics. More detail on eclipse geometry and the science of eclipses can be found by following the links from my website.

An *eclipse* occurs when one celestial body moves in front of another, blocking the light from the Sun. During a *lunar eclipse*, the Moon lines up behind the Earth, as seen from the Sun, and passes into the Earth's shadow. During a *solar eclipse*, the Moon moves between the Earth and the Sun. This blocks the light from the Sun from reaching the Earth, and the Moon's shadow is cast upon the Earth.

There are two parts to the Moon's shadow: the dark inner shadow (the *umbra*) and the lighter outer shadow (the *penumbra*). Viewing from Earth, if you are within the Moon's outer shadow, you will see a *partial solar eclipse*, with the Moon blocking only part of the Sun. If you are within the Moon's dark inner shadow, you will see a *total solar eclipse*—the greatest show on Earth. Every eighteen months or so, the Moon's inner shadow traces a narrow path across the Earth, allowing those within this *path of totality* to witness the majestic total solar eclipse.

A total solar eclipse starts with a partial eclipse. The Moon begins to block the Sun, and the lighter outer shadow of the Moon is cast over a wide region. For those within the path of totality, the show is only just beginning. Over time, the reduced light and heat from the Sun produces subtle changes in the environment. Eventually, the darker inner shadow arrives as the Moon fully blocks out the Sun, dramatically plunging those within the path into an eerie darkness. This moment—*totality*—usually lasts a few minutes. Day becomes a deep twilight, dark enough to see the brightest stars and planets above. It is an other-worldly experience that many people find difficult to describe.

Looking directly at the bright surface of the Sun can damage your eyes. To view a solar eclipse, you need to be aware of how to view safely, and detailed guidance on this is provided in section five. During the partial phases, *solar filters* must be used to view directly; and indirect methods can be employed such as projecting the image onto a card or in a box. However, totality can be viewed safely without filters, because the Sun's bright surface is completely blocked by the Moon. In fact, you will find it hard not to look, as you will be completely captivated and awestruck by what you see.

The Sun's atmosphere—the *corona*—becomes visible, and is one of the main features of totality. The corona looks like a wispy, ethereal light, and is no brighter than the full Moon. Other important features can be seen during totality, and two are worthy of mention for beginners. Immediately before totality, *Baily's beads* are visible—numerous beads of sunlight shining through multiple valleys on the Moon's limb. The *diamond ring* is the final bead of sunlight shining through a single deep valley on the Moon's limb. As the inner corona of the Sun also becomes visible around the rest of the Moon's limb, it does indeed take on the appearance of a ring suspended above. The diamond ring and Baily's beads occur again, marking the end of totality and the return of the brightness of the Sun. The Moon's central shadow then rushes away. The partial eclipse continues on for another hour or so, until the Moon no longer blocks any part of the Sun.

Many people have seen a partial eclipse; through solar filters it looks like a bite has been taken out of the Sun. But very few have seen a total solar eclipse. In any one location, they are extremely rare, occurring only once in 375 years on average. Only those within the path of totality will experience a total solar eclipse. Outside of this path, you will not experience the immersive impact of totality, nor will you see the awe-inspiring sights. You will only see a partial eclipse. There is no comparison.

If you are very lucky, you may find yourself living in the right place, at the right time, along a path of totality. If you are not that lucky, and most of us are not, then you have to travel to the path of totality. And this is exactly what us eclipse chasers do as often as we can.

Totality occurs because of a coincidence of scale. The diameter of the Moon is four hundred times smaller than the diameter of the Sun, which is four hundred times farther away from the Earth. This gives them the same apparent size, allowing the perfect alignment we see during a total eclipse. We are, in a historical sense, on the right planet at the right time to experience this celestial wonder. Over time, as the Moon moves away from the Earth, a total eclipse will no longer be visible. But don't panic—this won't happen for another 500 million years or so. There is time to see a few more yet.

The main feature of the total solar eclipse is totality. If you are not within the path of totality, you will not experience those moments of darkness with all the drama outlined earlier. You will only see a partial eclipse.

It is very hard to convey to people who have not experienced totality that a partial eclipse is nothing compared to a total eclipse. Being near to the path doesn't give you any of the unique features of totality. *You must be in the path.* This cannot be stressed enough.

Many analogies have been used to describe the difference between a partial and total eclipse. For example, it is like comparing a peck on the cheek to a night of passionate love. But I am going to describe the difference using one of my other passions: molten chocolate lava cake. Please bear with me!

To the uninitiated, a molten chocolate lava cake is one of the most sumptuous of desserts. It consists of a chocolate soufflé cake with a liquid chocolate center. If you are a chocolate lover, as I am, then you cannot get closer to perfection than this. I dream of molten chocolate lava cake.

Let us imagine you have just ordered a molten chocolate lava cake at a local restaurant. You hear noises in the kitchen and pick up some incredible aromas. Then the moment finally arrives: the waiter places your dessert in front of you. It looks incredible. You take a deep breath, and your eyes glaze over with the smell of chocolaty goodness. There are no words to describe what you are feeling at this moment. You break the dessert with your spoon and put the cake in your mouth. Your taste buds explode. It is sublime. You involuntarily make suggestive noises: "Oh, mmm, ahh." You cannot believe how good it tastes. With your next spoonful, the molten melted center oozes out, spilling around the plate. You scoop up some of this molten center, and it melts on your tongue. It. Is. So. Good. You savor it all—the smell, the texture, the taste. You never want the moment to end.

The total solar eclipse is like the above scenario: a rich, multisensory experience that gives you waves of pleasure and euphoria. In comparison, a partial eclipse is like seeing a photograph of a molten chocolate lava cake. You can identify what it is by the image, and nothing more. You *see* it, but you do not *experience* it.

Try not to settle for the partial eclipse when you have a chance to get into the path of totality to experience a total solar eclipse. It is nature's grandest spectacle, and one of life's most intense and stunning moments. Everyone can appreciate the experience, even if you are not a chocolate lover.

Anyone can learn the details, facts, and figures of a total solar eclipse. However, it is much harder to understand the experience of totality. This is why I have written this book.

Across the world, the total eclipse has inspired myths and legends. Many thought it was an omen of doom, signaling the end of the world. Written historical accounts of totality convey feelings of awe and terror but also wonder and admiration. In the present day, explanations and accurate predictions demystify the experience. Yet we still respond with primitive emotions that are a mix of awe, fear, and disbelief.

The eclipse experience is relevant to all regardless of age, background, or culture. Only through personal stories can we gain a unique insight into the wonder of what it is like being in the shadow of the Moon.

CHAPTER 2

EARTHLY BEINGS IN THE SHADOW

North Queensland is where I'm from, where my family still lives, and is the setting for our story. So you could say it's very close to my heart. North Queensland is a tropical paradise with unspoiled beaches, primary rainforests, volcanic history, and is on the doorstep of the Great Barrier Reef. The region is no stranger to dramatic nature events, usually in the form of tropical cyclones.

On November 14, 2012, it was the setting for the most sublime, awe-inspiring nature event in over one thousand years: the total solar eclipse.

The shadow of the Moon first made landfall in the remote and unpopulated Northern Territory at sunrise. It then swept across Far North Queensland before heading out to the Pacific Ocean, passing north of the North Island of New Zealand. The path of totality was 111 miles wide, from Innisfail to the south, and Bloomfield to the north. Around 120,000 people were lucky enough to be living within the path of totality. Sixty thousand people visited specifically for the eclipse, double the initial estimates. It was an unprecedented event in the tourist off-season, with hotels and car rentals at full capacity.

This eclipse created a unique double dawn. Sunrise along the coastal regions within the path occurred at 5:38 a.m., with the partial eclipse starting fewer than ten minutes later at 5:45 a.m. Totality started at 6:38 a.m., lasting a maximum of two minutes. The partial eclipse continued until 7:40 a.m.

The weather on eclipse morning was, as predicted, mostly clear at inland locations and mostly cloudy along the coast. Observers along the coast found clouds a key part of their experience, with the majority only catching glimpses of totality. Those who traveled inland were rewarded with a magnificent show under clear blue skies.

Let's now take a look at each of our beings in the shadow to provide a little context to their stories. These ordinary people describe what it is like to be in the right place at the right time to see their first total eclipse. Some lived within the path of totality, while others traveled into the path specifically for the event. Pseudonyms have been used for anonymity.

Who are these beings? What did they know about eclipses before the event? What were their expectations leading up to the eclipse? Follow them on their journey from the day before the eclipse, eclipse morning, during totality, and their insights in the weeks afterward.

I. CARA

A newlywed on her journey to a simple life

CARA WAS A SOFT-SPOKEN THIRTY-YEAR-OLD, with a tiny frame and long blonde hair. Having trained and practiced as a solicitor, Cara spent several years living in Brisbane with her partner Mike. They married and, for their honeymoon, traveled around Australia in their campervan.

In her earlier years, Cara had traveled to developing countries. Seeing the precarious nature of peace in other countries made her appreciate the stability of life in Australia. This influenced her choice of career. She also vowed that she would travel every year—regardless of her income—to connect to different ways of life.

After their intrepid honeymoon, Cara and Mike decided they wanted to live a life of simplicity and be closer to nature. They had just relocated to Tolga—a small town of two thousand in Far North Queensland—in the months before the eclipse. They had no idea that their new home was right within the path of totality for the total eclipse.

They settled in to their simpler life with ease. Their home sat on the edge of an ancient volcano, and they were growing their own vegetables. They didn't have much in the way of material things: no TV and only basic furniture. They felt like grandma and grandpa—spending their time together, listening to the radio at night, and reading. They couldn't have been happier.

A few weeks after arriving in the region, Cara learned that a total eclipse was going to be visible from their town. She recalled using a cardboard box for eclipse-viewing as a child, and had more recently seen a news report of people using a similar box to view the transit of Venus. She assumed the total eclipse would be a similar event, and shrugged it off. Unlike her husband, she was not into scientific or astronomical events.

As the eclipse drew nearer, media reports focused on how eclipse tourists would bring a much-needed economic boom to the region. Eclipse information was given, and the repeated messages on eye safety reinforced Cara's view that it was a box experience. It was an event happening in the region, yes, but remained of no real particular interest to her.

Two weeks before the eclipse, Cara paid closer attention to media reports. She now understood the need to be within the path of totality and how to view safely with solar filters. She went along to the nearby tourist office to get her eclipse glasses, along with a map of the path of totality. To her, the eclipse remained a way of sharing a common experience within the community, rather than one of personal interest.

That changed, however, when Cara heard me speak on the radio about my personal eclipse experiences. Hearing the passion in my voice, Cara learned that the total eclipse could be enjoyed by everyone, and was not just an astronomical event. For the first time, she wondered, *What would it be like for the world to go dark for those few moments of totality?*

From that moment, the eclipse stirred up a curiosity and energy that she wanted to share. She took pictures of herself with her eclipse glasses, beaming widely, and shared them with family and friends living outside of the path. They all noted how similar the glasses were to early 3D glasses used at cinemas as a child. Her own family felt just like she had initially felt: expressing little interest in the eclipse. But she found her husband's friends—those who had an interest in the sciences—expressing excitement. Some were talking about traveling to join them for the eclipse.

Living within the path of totality, Cara knew they would be able to see the full eclipse from their home. But she now wanted to turn the eclipse into an overnight campervan adventure. She sought local opinion on the best places to view the early-morning eclipse. Those not staying home had the same plan: to watch the sunrise and then the total eclipse from a spectacular lookout fifteen miles to the north. For Cara, it was the perfect overnight camping spot, although she was a little concerned by the numbers planning to view from that location. But the plan was made. Her eyes lit up every time she thought about seeing her very first total solar eclipse—without a box.

As eclipse day grew closer, she struggled to keep the nervous anticipation inside. She bounced around with endless energy, and all thoughts centered on one thing and one thing only: the eclipse was coming.

II. PETER

A storm-chaser seeking a private moment with the Universe

PETER, AGE THIRTY-FIVE, WAS A friendly guy with a small frame and a large smile. He worked as a freelance videographer, reporting on weather stories for the local and state TV news. His base in Townsville was three hours south of the path of totality, but his work covered the whole of North Queensland.

Peter grew up in an isolated community in the remote west of the Far North Queensland peninsula. Growing up in such a remote location made him feel connected to nature from a young age. He developed a love of weather, which then turned into an obsession with severe weather and cyclones.

Five years before the eclipse, Peter was work-oriented, stressed, and burnt out. The sudden death of his close friend shocked him, and soon after this, he experienced a crisis in his own health. These events were a turning point. He realized that you never know when your time is up. It was time for him to make important and meaningful life choices. Following his recovery, he traveled around Australia alone in his land cruiser, thinking about his life and how he wanted things to be. He wanted to chase storms. Big storms. He finally went to the US to live his dream of chasing tornadoes.

Peter spent several seasons tornado chasing and working as part of a tour company. His new focus was on appreciating everyday beauty. He developed an interest in alternative therapies, yoga, and healthy eating. He recognized that since slowing down the pace, his life was so much more enriched and he was much happier.

While in the US chasing tornadoes in early 2012, Peter's group was mesmerized by a partially eclipsed sunset. The unexpected celestial alignment caught him by surprise, and piqued his interest for future photography.

When Peter first learned that a total solar eclipse would be visible in Far North Queensland, he knew he would document it. He planned to observe it from a scenic outlook in Townsville, well outside of the path of totality, giving a 96 percent partial eclipse. He expected it to be like his prior sunset eclipse, although this one would occur soon after sunrise. It never occurred to him that remaining outside of the path of totality meant he would miss his chance of experiencing something so much more.

He only questioned his plan when he heard me talk about the total eclipse experience on the radio and TV. Recognizing my passion and excitement from his own tornado chasing, he decided he *must* drive a few hours north into the path of totality. He knew the region well and was also familiar with the weather patterns, having chased storms in the region for decades. He would not let this opportunity pass him by. His only restriction was time. He was due to work later that day in Townsville, so he would have to travel back as soon as the eclipse ended.

Peter arranged an overnight trip on his own. His focus was to document the total eclipse, and enjoy the experience. He wanted to find a location where he was away from crowds. But he also knew that the weather was a key consideration— if it was cloudy, he would miss it.

As a local storm-chaser, he knew clouds were a feature of the early-morning coastal weather. Peter knew he would find clearer skies in the remote interior, and began making plans with methodical precision. He studied satellite and radar images as well as GPS coordinates of different roads and four-wheel drive tracks within the path of totality. His ultimate aim was to get as close to the centerline—the middle of the path of totality—as possible.

He ensured his location was south of a turn-off to the Eclipse Festival, with an estimated crowd of ten thousand people. This would give him a chance to avoid the worst of the post-eclipse traffic. He prepared his land cruiser to ensure he was self-sufficient, allowing him to pull off anywhere on the side of the road in isolation.

Peter knew from his tornado-chasing and storm-chasing that high adrenaline had the potential to interfere with videography. Although he could not see how the total eclipse would be high adrenaline, he planned for it anyway. He wanted to experience the eclipse directly, and not from behind a camera lens. He set up two brackets for his camera so they could run without his involvement.

Finally, after much planning, he was ready to chase this eclipse. A little voice in his head told him that this might be something very special.

III. TABITHA

A creative dreamer organizing the perfect eclipse family reunion

TABITHA, A TALL AND ATHLETIC-LOOKING twenty-eight-year-old with short black hair, grew up within the path of totality with her mother and sister. She worked in information technology, although she enjoyed creative activities such as writing songs and performing intimate gigs.

Tabitha always believed that the Far North Queensland region was a special place. The rainforest had a unique energy. Her family still lived in the region, while she was now based over two thousand miles farther south in Tasmania.

She had an eclectic background, having studied history and archaeology. She had an interest in spirituality and science fiction and, along with her mother, shared a passion for ancient civilizations. She described herself as a perfectionist, always wanting to make sure things were *just right*.

Tabitha and her mother were fascinated with the ending of one of the long count cycles of the ancient Mayan calendar in the year 2012. When they also learned that a total solar eclipse was going to be visible in their region in 2012, the coincidence was too much to ignore. The three of them—Tabitha, her mother, and her sister—agreed to all come together to experience the eclipse in this auspicious year and reflect on their lives.

In the years leading up to 2012, the family would reconnect and talk excitedly about how important the eclipse in 2012 was going to be.

And then, the year Tabitha had waited her whole adult life for had finally arrived. As she saw in the New Year, she did not expect to start feeling anxious about the eclipse and its meaning. She dreamed about trying to see the eclipse, but things kept getting in the way. To her, it was more than just an eclipse. The anticipation of this special year, and this special eclipse, made it so important.

Tabitha arrived in Far North Queensland about two weeks before the eclipse. She wanted to know what it would be like to view the sunrise and eclipse from their preferred viewing location at Wonga Beach. For several days in a row, she woke up at 5:00 a.m. and drove to Wonga Beach. She sat on the beach, watching the sunrise, and stayed until 7:00

a.m., trying to get a feel for what eclipse morning would be like. Every day, thick clouds muddled her view.

Talking to eclipse chasers, Tabitha learned of the extreme lengths taken to ensure the best view along the path of totality. She realized she didn't have to play it safe by remaining in locations they knew. She started exploring options for viewing away from the coast and farther inland, where weather prospects were better.

Tabitha drove inland to Lakeland Downs, around one hundred miles to the west, to do a dress rehearsal for eclipse day. She set up camp on her own, feeling very proud of the research she completed to ensure the family would have the best eclipse reunion. As she woke early to watch the sunrise the following day, clear skies greeted her and stuck around the whole morning. Her search for the perfect location for their very special family event was over.

IV. SIMON

An English backpacker living for each moment

SIMON, AGE THIRTY-ONE, COULDN'T HAVE been farther away from his home in England if he tried. He had a disheveled look about him, with a typical laidback hippy attitude. He appeared warm and authentic. He spoke like one would imagine a backpacker would speak, peppering his words with, "Yeah, man" and "Like, totally awesome."

Simon loved seeking out new experiences, especially natural wonders. Backpacking his way around the world, his last two years were spent enjoying Australia's unique landscapes. He picked up work whenever he could, supplementing his income to keep traveling.

His ill mother raised him through childhood and urged him to grab life with both hands, to enjoy every moment, and to be grateful for his health. After she died when he was in his early teens, he held on to those beliefs. He knew how life could be over so quickly, and how important it was to be in the present. Although he was currently carefree with few responsibilities, he imagined a more stable future with a family. But, for the current time, he lived in the moment.

In the past year, Simon had been inspired by a lunar eclipse and the transit of Venus. Now, he was about to experience a total solar eclipse. It couldn't get better than this, and he was happy to be in the right country at the right time to experience this natural wonder.

Simon had always loved nature, and enjoyed learning about science and the planets at school. He also enjoyed science fiction movies, and was fascinated with the Universe.

In 1999, the path of totality went across the south of England. Fifteen at the time, Simon traveled into the path of totality to attend the Eclipse Festival with his friends. Unfortunately, heavy clouds blocked the view at his location and across most of the path in the south of England. He recalled the rapid transition from light to dark and then light again, and wanted to experience the full eclipse under clear skies. He learned soon after arriving to Australia that the total eclipse was happening, and he decided that he was meant to go.

Simon temporarily worked in Perth, over three thousand miles away on the other side of the country. He met Tabitha, the reunion-planner, the year before, and had learned of her plans to view this special eclipse with her family. Although it wasn't the most sensible financial decision, Simon felt he *had* to be there and planned to fly into the region to join the family.

Simon knew the total solar eclipse was something special. He wouldn't have missed it for the world.

V. TERRY

A reflective local wanting to party with ten thousand other festival-goers

TERRY WAS A TWENTY-TWO-YEAR-OLD CHEF from Clifton Beach near Cairns, with short curly hair and a broad smile. Working long and stressful hours as a chef in a luxury resort, he had a passion for cooking and food. Although chilled and laidback, Terry kept his mind active with learning. He was self-aware, expressing maturity not usually present in those of his age. He enjoyed conversations about life and philosophy. He was confident about his own ideas, even if they differed from his peers. But he still enjoyed going out and partying when he could.

During his first scuba-dive as a teenager, he became fascinated by the undersea world. It seemed so alien to life above the water. The experience led to a curiosity in the reef, science, biology, and conservation. This then developed further into an interest in the world and the Universe. Traveling to developing countries made him realize that he was lucky in his life circumstances. He had a dream to go traveling to live more in the moment, while volunteering to do something meaningful.

Terry first heard about the eclipse at the start of the year in conversations at work. He thought the eclipse would be an interesting thing to see, due to his interest in space. But most around him didn't see it as interesting. Instead, the focus was on the increased tourism at the resort at a normally quiet time of year.

Some weeks later, his artist and DJ friends told him about the large Eclipse Festival they were attending. An inland rural property was hosting the festival, with an expected crowd of ten thousand. Researching the festival online, Terry figured it would be a great place to party, and booked his tickets. It met his needs perfectly. He was due a break from work at that time, he could party with his friends, and he could meet new people. While the festival vibe was the main draw, the eclipse felt like a good bonus.

As the eclipse drew near, Terry learned that tens of thousands of people were expected in his home beach location. And his work resort at Palm Cove was near the chosen location for the major live broadcasts for the eclipse. Yet he would be 230 miles inland, at the festival with thousands of others—from one crowd to another. He couldn't wait.

VI. ROSE

A single mother currently restricted by life circumstances

ROSE, A THIRTY-YEAR-OLD SINGLE MOTHER, was a secondary school teacher in Cairns. She would shyly tuck her mid-length brown hair behind her ears as she spoke. She was born and raised in Cairns, the main city in the path of totality. Growing up, she enjoyed snorkeling on the reef and had a passion for travel and adventure. Having learned Japanese in primary school, she developed a fascination with Japanese culture. She then spent two years teaching in Japan, charmed by the people and way of life. She longed to return, but her life circumstances changed when her son, now five, was born. After raising him for several years, she worked in banking but had recently returned to teaching.

Rose first became aware of the eclipse the previous November. She assumed it was only of relevance to scientists and astronomers, and had no interest in the eclipse. In the months leading up to the eclipse, her secondary school was often featured in the media with eclipse-related news. They hosted guest speakers and shared information about safe solar viewing.

Rose was the teacher assigned to selling eclipse glasses at the school fundraiser. She answered questions as best as she could but knew very little about the eclipse. Her interest increased when she sat in on a lecture that featured a simulation of the total eclipse. Seeing what it may look like made it feel so much more real to her. In fact, it made her feel like she did years before, when she had the freedom to travel. Listening to news reports and personal stories aroused her interest even more, and she became giddy. She wanted to experience it all, from sunrise through to totality and beyond.

Rose knew the ideal spot to view the sunrise and the total eclipse. This would be from the top of Glacier Rock, a distinctive local feature fifteen miles to the south with fantastic views to the east. But it would involve trekking up in the dark before sunrise with her five-year-old son. She did seriously consider this option but felt the climb in the dark in the wet season would be too difficult.

The other complication was the pressure to start work on time; there were no exceptions. For the locals, eclipse day was a normal working day, as the whole eclipse was over by 9:00 a.m. This restricted her options for viewing, as she needed to be nearby to avoid any potential traffic issues.

The week before the eclipse, she asked her mother to wake early and view sunrise from the balcony of her home a few streets away. Her mother confirmed a clear view of the sunrise, which continued throughout the time of the eclipse. Rose then decided this would be the best plan: viewing together as a family from her mother's balcony. She could avoid driving and the risk of getting caught in any potential traffic hotspots. Having made this decision, she couldn't wait for eclipse day, almost feeling like a child again waiting for her birthday.

Rose wondered what the darkness of totality would be like. She enjoyed walking at dusk, watching the change of light before returning in the dark, and imagined it would be something similar. It seemed strange to think about having sudden darkness so soon after sunrise.

Hearing her son talk nonstop about the eclipse and what he learned at school fueled her own desire to learn about it. As eclipse day got closer, she obsessively watched every news report, desperate not to miss a thing. Nothing else mattered—and she felt alive in a way she hadn't felt for years.

2

INTO THE PATH

CHAPTER 3

TOTALITY MINUS ONE

Tuesday, November 13, 2012, the day before the total eclipse, started as a typical hot and humid summer day. Locals were stirring early, getting ready for their day. In the fully booked hotels, tourists packed their gear, ready to start their adventures of exploring the region's many attractions. Farther inland, the Eclipse Festival was already in its third day. It was a celebration of sound, lights, and color building up to the total eclipse.

Many listened to the morning news on the radio or watched local TV to get further updates about the early-morning eclipse. Interviews with international travelers arriving in the region revealed their passion and excitement. Locals were now also eagerly awaiting what the next day would bring. Many were planning breakfast celebrations within their own homes with family and friends.

There was a palpable feeling of energy and enthusiasm. Never before was it so busy in November in the tropical north. There was no escaping the fact that something big was about to happen. This time, instead of it being a destructive nature event, it was to be a rare celestial alignment. But one question weighed heavy on everyone's minds: would it be cloudy on eclipse day?

I. CARA

The Newlywed

IT WAS THE AFTERNOON OF November 13, the day before the eclipse. Cara whistled and sang as she prepared for their overnight camping trip. The radio was on, and when the detailed report of eclipse updates came on, she raced over to the radio and turned it up as loud as it could go. She heard me talk about what to expect on eclipse day if it were cloudy and if skies were clear. She hung on every word, her pulse raising. She could *feel* the anticipation coursing through her veins.

Mike arrived home early from work, looking concerned. He had been studying the weather forecasts and had been talking to others about their plans. Getting the maps out, Mike argued that they should make a last-minute change and head even farther north, where clearer weather was predicted. He wanted to get as close to the center of the path of totality as possible, stressing the location with his finger tapping on the map. The urgency of this decision, and the build-up from the radio, was too much for Cara. Taking a deep breath in, she squealed with glee as she bounced up and down. "Yes, let's do it!" she said, clapping wildly. They hugged, jumping up and down together, whooping with joy. Their dog Yoda picked up on the vibe and joined in too, barking and jumping on them.

Suddenly, everything was all go. They packed up the final bits in their camper and called a few family members to let them know of their plans. Then it was time. They locked the house, called Yoda into the back of the camper, and started their journey. They stopped in at their regular gas station to get fuel and shared their new plans, wishing everyone a happy eclipse.

North of Mareeba, they encountered heavy traffic, heading both north and south. The Mulligan Highway was the main access for the ten thousand people attending the Eclipse Festival as well as everyone who had chosen to view from an inland location. Cara was not stressed by this—instead, it made her feel even more a part of something special that was building up with every passing moment. She could not stop smiling.

As they approached the pub at Mount Carbine, the nearest services to the centerline, they noted campervans everywhere. They wanted to stop to soak up the atmosphere, but they were also eager to find an isolated spot to camp before dark. Driving farther north, they saw people had set up camps and cameras on either side of the road to be in position for the following morning. They had never seen anything like it.

They continued along until they noticed a narrow dirt track off the main highway, leading up to a hill. Taking the turn, they then drove up the long, narrow dirt path until they found a suitable spot to camp for the night. They got out their compass, ensured they had a view to the east, and then leveled out the camper. Once they were in their position and set up for the evening, the excitement overtook them and they were jumping up and down yet again. Even Yoda followed suit. They turned on the local radio to hear interviews from the eclipse media event earlier in the day. They couldn't quite believe there were so many people arriving to view this celestial event, and they felt lucky to be living here and being a part of it all.

Looking around, they could see people and cars all over the hillside and beyond. All had set up their impromptu camps amidst the harsh Australian outback. As darkness descended, the camps flickered lights below them as the stars above dazzled. The whole scene was so moving and unexpected that Cara wept tears of happiness. She felt goosebumps at being part of so many coming together, all on this rural land to see a celestial event. This was so far away from what she had initially thought it would be, viewing through a box. She laughed at how naive she had been.

Even though they were alone in their location, they were a part of something so much greater. Cara was too excited to sleep, but eventually settled in to the sounds of nature all around, with Mike and Yoda by her side.

II. PETER

The Storm-Chaser

AT 8:00 A.M. ON THE morning of November 13, the day before the eclipse, Peter set off from Townsville heading north for the path of totality. He had packed his land cruiser the previous night, ready for an early departure. He would camp for one night, although he was prepared for serious travel disruption. He knew he had made the right choice to drive into the path of totality, to experience the total eclipse. The planning and research reminded him of chasing a storm, except this time he was chasing the Moon's shadow. He liked that idea.

Peter was creating a documentary of his eclipse chase, and had mounted his camera on the dashboard of the cruiser to make this easier. Once he cleared the city morning traffic and reached Bruce Highway, he recorded some of his thoughts.

After driving for several hours, Peter cheered as he crossed into the path of totality. He was going to experience the full total solar eclipse! He made a video entry, and suddenly it all felt real. Around twenty minutes later, he passed through Tolga, where Cara busily prepared for their own trip north along the same highway.

A steady stream of traffic flowed on the remote highway, and Peter smiled as he praised himself for being self-sufficient and fueling up before he entered the path of totality. He had no need to stop at the small gas station and pub at Mount Carbine, which was already overwhelmed with queues of vehicles.

Having now been on the road for over six hours, he kept an eye out for places to camp. He wanted a location where the mountains were not going to block sunrise. He wanted to explore Bob's Lookout, at the top of the Desailly Range, which overlooked a fantastic savannah landscape toward the coast. It would be perfect for his documentary and for viewing the eclipse.

He stopped at the Lookout car park, stretched his legs, and took in the spectacular sweeping view. He noticed about ten vehicles camped at the top and recognized Sun-tracking devices amidst the telescopes and cameras, prepped and ready for the eclipse the following day. Peter figured these people knew what they were doing. Keeping this in mind, and noting the time was 4:30 p.m., he gave himself another hour to scout a little farther north for a more isolated spot. With nothing rivaling the outlook from Bob's Lookout, he returned, taking a more detailed look for a camping spot for his land cruiser. He noticed a quiet spot below the lookout summit, which was far enough off the road to be safe to camp. Just him and the Universe.

Once he parked, Peter efficiently got to work setting up his rooftop tent and preparing his table and chair space around the vehicle. He then sat back with a cold bottle of beer, relishing in spending time alone in the outback as he had done so many times in the past. He could finally relax. From his elevated position, he could see the road with the steady flow of traffic coming in from the coast. He had expected it to be busy, and was glad he arrived when he did.

As darkness set in, Peter noted the traffic increasing. People in the thousands were coming inland. All seemed to be doing the same as him: finding a space to pull over and camp overnight.

After a full day of driving, Peter retired to his rooftop tent, ready for an early night and a bit of peace and reflection under a canopy of stars. But after settling in, the sound and lights from the steady stream of traffic were irritating. Little did he know that it would only become worse as the night wore on.

Peter had expected to be viewing and recording the eclipse in isolation. However, his location under Bob's Lookout was, in fact, a magnet for everyone arriving at the last moment. Vehicle after vehicle pulled up close to where he was parked. Many people encroached on his campsite, shining lights on his tent, talking loudly, and smoking. It was not quite the nature experience he had hoped for.

And still they came. More people arrived, parking and walking around in the dark, trying to find their spot amongst the existing camps. He could hear vehicles running to power the air-conditioning, and his tent filled with fumes.

Despite his meticulous planning, Peter had failed to account for the crowds. Wearily, he got up, acknowledging that he wasn't going to get a restful night's sleep. He needed to ensure he had the space around him for his videography. Using his head lamp, he placed equipment and a kit around his vehicle, ensuring his space was protected. He returned to his tent, watching the comings-and-goings of the new arrivals. In the early hours, he tried to get a little sleep before his alarm would wake him at 4:00 a.m.

III. TABITHA

The Reunion-Planner

THE MORNING OF THE DAY before the eclipse, Tabitha woke up and prepared for yet another day of fun socializing with her family and friends. Many of her friends had also returned home for the eclipse, making it a very enjoyable time. Never before had it felt so thrilling to be back.

Yet she frowned every time she thought about the eclipse. She needed the clouds to stay away—their family eclipse gathering had to be *just* right. Had she made the best choice? Her mind ticked over all the possibilities, and she felt weighed down by it all. She wondered how eclipse chasers managed the uncertainty of not knowing, especially in the absence of local knowledge.

She collected Simon, her backpacker friend, from the airport. Hundreds of people crowded the airport, busier compared to the previous fortnight when she had arrived. Gathering their final supplies and belongings, Tabitha and her family packed up the cars in preparation for their journey inland to Lakeland. She looked up final weather reports, and then they started on their journey. Once over the range, clear blue skies replaced the gray, coastal ones. Tabitha knew they had made the right decision to head inland.

Arriving at Lakeland, things looked the same as it had a few days before on her solo scouting trip. Except this time, there were many more people. Leaving her family to freshen up after the drive, Tabitha and Simon walked around to see how others were preparing their sites. She saw eclipse chasers with cameras and telescopes. She chatted with two couples attending the Eclipse Festival, and a couple who had driven up from Sydney, over 1,600 miles away. There were some odd sights. There was a man wearing a full suit in the heat of the outback summer. Never before had she seen such an eclectic group of people come together to camp!

They returned to their own site, trying to figure how best to set things up. Tabitha looked toward the eastern horizon and placed her outstretched fists together, estimating where the eclipsed Sun would be at totality. Making sure they maximized this view, they set up their tents, blankets, and chairs.

Once the camp was set up, all that was left was to make a cup of tea. Whatever was happening in her life, Tabitha stuck to the ritual of making a cup of tea. It made her feel like everything was going to be okay.

Everyone gathered around, catching up with stories of dreams and goals. Tabitha finally sat down on her folding camp chair, relaxing with a cup of tea in her hand. She took a deep breath in, closing her eyes, taking in the moment. They had done it—all together for this special event, as they had been planning for most of her adult life. She let out a huge sigh of relief, opening her eyes to take in everyone gathered together. Her mom sat in front of her, smiling proudly. Her sister entertained her young niece. Her friend Simon sat next to her, happy to be sharing this experience with them. All the planning was now over. She settled in and enjoyed the moment with her loved ones.

The intimate moment was broken, though, when a car came driving up and parked right beside them—even though there were spaces farther away. As a group, they expressed their irritation at the intrusion of their private space. An older couple got out, smiled, and prepared their campsite right next to them. After a few moments of glaring looks, they engaged in small talk and relaxed when they learned more about this interesting couple. They had chased several eclipses, and were full of information and stories. Tabitha let go of her protective demeanor, and welcomed the couple to share in with the conversations.

As the evening progressed, Tabitha figured they had achieved their family goal of coming together for the eclipse. Whatever happened—even if clouds obscured the eclipse— they were together, in the path of totality. And there was tea.

Later that evening, Tabitha fell asleep, exhausted. She awoke and saw the dazzling stars above her, feeling reassured before drifting off to sleep again. She dreamed that she was driving to see the eclipse, but it was always out of sight, over the next hill.

IV. SIMON

The Backpacker

ON THE DAY BEFORE THE eclipse, Simon arrived at the Cairns Airport. He had flown in from Perth, on the other side of the country. The airport bustled with people flooding into the region specifically for the eclipse. He had left behind the opportunity to earn money, which he needed, to come for the eclipse. It wasn't the best timing, but he knew there was no price for an experience like this. He would worry about the impact of his decision later.

Tabitha wrapped her arms around him, and he shared how grateful he was to join her and her family for this meaningful eclipse. He could tell she was anxious even though there was a plan. She worried about things she had no control over, such as the weather.

He met the rest of the family, and then they all set off in their little convoy. The drive up over the range and up to Lakeland was pretty uneventful, and Simon spent most of it chatting or sleeping.

He enjoyed walking around the area after they arrived, meeting people from all over the world. He thought there was something pretty cool about random people from so many different places all coming to the same location. But now, sitting with a cup of tea in his hand, he relaxed with the world. He could feel Tabitha finally relaxing too, recognizing that all the planning was over. He was glad that she could let go of feeling responsible for everyone else. He had learned early on in life that some things happen and you have no control over them and you have to let it go.

It was then with some irony that this worldview was challenged when the older couple intruded on their personal space. But seeing a life lesson in everything, Simon recognized they were rewarded by opening up to these new people.

Simon went to sleep thinking about how this eclipse was going to be different to what little he remembered from his 1999 eclipse experience. He did recall it going dark, but not much else. Back then, his main focus was on partying with his friends. Simon realized how much he had matured since then.

V. TERRY

The Festival-Goer

ON NOVEMBER 13, THE DAY before the eclipse, Terry was still struggling with the dry, intense heat. Standing under the stage sprinklers at the Eclipse Festival, and then catching the light breeze, at least took the edge off to make things more bearable. Apart from managing the heat, Terry was feeling at home on day three of the festival. He had attended some of the talks and activities arranged to share wisdom on all aspects of life. He figured it wasn't for him. He already had a good sense of how things worked and didn't need to be told about mysteries of the world. He spent his time dancing to the music—hard work in the heat. When he wasn't dancing or cooling off, Terry sat back and observed his fellow attendees with amused interest. He saw a girl dressed as a rainbow, with bright ribbons in her hair and strong metallic colors on her eyelids. She would often sit in the middle of the dance area, eyes closed and goofy smile on her face. Then there was Gandalf, a seventy-year-old man straight out of Woodstock, complete with Technicolor shirt and long beard. Some he had encountered were a little *reality-challenged*, but most people were chilled and relaxed. Everyone was there to have a good time, to experience the eclipse, and to connect with others.

His artist and DJ friends were part of the festival program. He could come and go from their base, which helped him meet a wide range of new people. It made his festival experience especially enjoyable.

The evenings were cooler, and easier to get into the festival vibe, with rainbow-colored lighting accentuating the impressive structures. It looked like a fairytale land.

That evening, Terry stepped away from the brightly lit festival stages and took a moment to appreciate the darkness. He looked up in awe at the twinkling stars above. Very soon, the Sun and the Moon were going to be in alignment. He was aware that many others were planning an all-nighter, waiting for sunrise and then the eclipse. That was not *his* plan. He wanted to be fully present to enjoy the experience. So, after partying with his friends, he returned to his tent at 2:00 a.m. so he could recharge for three hours. He didn't want to miss it.

VI. ROSE

The Wishful Teacher

THE DAY BEFORE THE ECLIPSE started like any other for Rose in Cairns. She was teaching her usual classes, but all she wanted to do was listen to eclipse news. Her teaching colleagues discussed their plans and expressed frustration at having to avoid potential traffic gridlock immediately following the eclipse. As they could not travel far for the eclipse, all they could do was hope the weather—and the traffic—would remain clear where they were.

After school, Rose stopped off to get some supplies for the following morning. She noticed the population seemed to have tripled since that morning. A part of her still longed to be able to see the eclipse somewhere exotic or more interesting. But she didn't have to worry about anything. She knew it would be a special day and wanted her family to be together. On hearing that her son's father no longer had to work, she invited him to join them too. It would be an important day for her son, and she wanted him to have good family memories.

She then spent more time searching for news on what was happening all over the north. She especially enjoyed hearing from the tourists coming from around the world to view the eclipse. She loved hearing their stories and wished she too could follow her desires. But she was lucky. Everyone had to travel to her home region—her little patch of the world—to see this amazing event. Living here gave her this unique opportunity to see something amazing. All she had to do the following morning was walk around the corner to her mother's house.

CHAPTER 4

ECLIPSE DAY

On Woody Isles, five miles off the Far North Queensland coast, the arrival of dawn came with a cacophony of sound. Thousands of pied imperial pigeons roosting in the trees began to stir. At first light, they took off in unison with screeches and shrieks, flying toward the mainland to hunt for the day.

Humans were also stirring across the region. Many had already made their way to numerous beaches to observe the sunrise. Some were located at the coast near to Woody Isles and were lucky to watch the arrival of the huge flock of pigeons in the early-morning skies above.

But this was no ordinary day. Eclipse day had finally arrived.

No sooner had the Sun started to warm up the land than the light was starting to dim. For the pigeons, the signal to return home to roost had begun. They again took off in their thousands, shrieking as they circled over the beaches before heading away from the coast. By the time they arrived back on Woody Isles, as they do at every sunset, panic set in as some broke out of the flock, unsure what to do. With suddenness, darkness fell. The birds silenced. And then, within moments, daylight suddenly returned again. The birds' confusion was clear as they made startled screeches at this unexpected second dawn. For the second time that morning, the huge noisy flock took flight toward the mainland.

How could they possibly understand the circumstances of this unique day of the double dawn?

I. CARA

The Newlywed

CARA LAY HALF ASLEEP IN the van's small bed. Memories of their recent honeymoon trip around Australia flooded back as she curled up on her familiar bed sheets. She focused on the bird and insect chirps, which were so loud that they almost drowned out the other camp noises. She heard Yoda moving about, and Mike making coffee, his movements gently rocking the van. Her mind was at peace, and she didn't want the moment to end.

Mike leaned against the bed beside her, asking her if she had already taken a look. She wiped her eyes and tried to focus on what was in the palm of his hand. Eclipse glasses. Suddenly, she recalled what day it was—eclipse day! She startled awake, grabbing the glasses, and leaned forward so she could see. She put her eclipse glasses on, and to her surprise noted that not only had she missed sunrise, but she had also missed the start of the eclipse! The Moon was already covering one-third of the Sun.

There was no way she would have known there was a partial eclipse happening without her eclipse glasses. She couldn't quite believe it. She had wrongly assumed they would be in the shade, as if a cloud were blocking the Sun. But it was still so bright.

Cara felt a little guilty about missing the start of the show, and for sleeping in so long. But Mike had everything under control. She watched for a few moments more from the bed, taking small glances through her solar filters. She then joined Mike on the picnic rug he had laid out. They sat there, pouring some local sparkling mango wine into their special wedding silver champagne glasses. It was, of course, a special occasion worthy of the best. They clinked their glasses to their life and to the experience that was about to unfold.

They had chosen their viewing site well. They were alone and the sky was completely clear. Through her eclipse glasses, she saw with each passing minute more and more of the Sun was being covered. The eclipse progressed faster than she had expected, and the world shifted around her. Yoda seemed oblivious to these changes, eager to fetch sticks. She noticed the subtle changes in light. She wasn't sure, but she thought the shadows were starting to change in a way that she hadn't noticed before. It was getting dimmer, and she noticed the air around her becoming cooler.

Nothing prepared her for the sudden change in the world around her and the arrival of the darkness of the Moon's shadow. Her senses were completely thrown. She could no longer see anything through her eclipse glasses and knew it was now safe to look without filters. Totality! They were in darkness and the eclipsed Sun was there like an eerie eye looking at her. She stared back, in awe.

Then Mike freaked out.

Mike had a science background and knew logically that totality was safe to view. He could no longer see anything through his filters. Yet when he stole a quick glance without his filters, the eclipsed Sun looked unlike anything he had ever seen before. In the moment, it all felt wrong and he panicked, convinced it wasn't safe to look. Repeated strong warnings in the media made him full of doubt and confusion. Could he *really* look straight at it? He heard a voice screaming out not to look—and realized it was him.

Cara knew her husband well. But at that moment, he was like a different person—unsure of himself and what to do. He said one thing and did another. He sneaked a peek at the eclipsed Sun, while yelling at her not to look.

Knowing that those precious seconds were ticking away, she put her foot down. She screamed at him: "Stop it! I'm looking—that is my choice!" She took a few steps forward, leaving him with his inner turmoil of not wanting to burn his eyes but being unable to look away. Cara knew it was safe and wanted to take in every single moment of totality.

The eclipsed Sun had a ring with flames, alive and moving. She figured that must be the corona. To her, it looked like a glowing ember of bluish silver light. It was amazing and beautiful. But it was scary too. She was unsure if it were due to Mike's panic and their interaction, or whether it was because it was so otherworldly.

Glancing around, Cara stood in a manipulated environment where things had gone haywire. The light was wrong. The darkness was wrong. The change of temperature was wrong. *This*, she thought, *was how you would dress the set of a movie for the end of the world.*

Then she looked at Mike, cowering behind her, peering through his fingers that were plastered onto his face. "Its all right, you can look," she said. And he did, letting out a strange *whoa*. His noise broke the silence—it was as if the sounds of nature had also stopped when the Sun disappeared. The sudden silence was wrong. Right at that moment, the silence was as chilling as a piercing scream.

She returned her gaze to the eclipsed Sun, unable to comprehend the darkness. It wasn't as dark or serene as at night; yet it wasn't like a normal dusk or twilight. How was it possible that she could see stars, when fewer than two hours ago the Sun had risen? A part of her still didn't believe it. Yet there she was, standing there and seeing with her own eyes. Illumination was coming from around the eclipsed Sun and, unusually, also from around the horizon. The world, now eerie, looked the wrong color.

She wondered what would happen if you were going about your daily life, and then suddenly a total eclipse occurred without warning. She imagined the terror, the chaos.

She turned to Mike again and found him taking a few photos, his mouth wide open in amazement. They hugged and lit sparklers to mark that special moment together. She noticed Yoda was unresponsive to these changes around them. He just wanted to be part of the action.

Cara also felt that her perception of time had changed— the eclipse went on forever, as if they were suspended in time. There was time to panic, to take it all in, to tell Yoda to go away, to look at the stars, to light the sparklers, and to take a few photos. She didn't understand how that could be, knowing totality was only two minutes long. But then, suddenly, the light returned in place of where the darkness had been. Time had started again, and totality was over.

Cara felt like she had been holding her breath the whole time. As totality ended, she heard herself, in perfect unison with Mike, utter a long *Whoaaa*. They looked at each other, dumbstruck, asking, "What just happened?" Confused, she didn't know quite what to do with herself. Yoda just wanted to fetch more sticks. She wondered if she could witness this today, what was possible for tomorrow? It was an unsettling thought.

Along with the return of the light came the sounds of nature, like the world was waking up from a slumber. She could again hear birds and insects, now a deafening sound. The world looked as bright as usual, even though the Sun remained mostly covered. Desperation to experience totality again overwhelmed her. She loved it! She so wanted to see it again, to hear it, to relive it, to ensure she would not forget the details.

She started yelling for totality to come back, but the creatures all around her drowned her out. Perhaps they were screaming out in confusion too.

II. PETER

The Storm-Chaser

LIKE MANY OTHERS IN THE region that morning, Peter awoke to his alarm at 4:00 a.m. Moving quietly, he left his tent and prepared himself a morning coffee. He had spent many mornings like this, waking early, camped in his vehicle at some remote location to watch the sunrise alone. But on this day, thousands of others joined him. Peter acknowledged that this was not going to be the private eclipse experience he had planned for. He was merely one human being observing this dance between the Sun and the Moon. He accepted he would have to be social given the circumstances—his nearest neighbors were so close they kept inadvertently making eye contact.

The sunrise from his location, overlooking the outback, was spectacular. Beautiful colors painted the land in quick succession. The heat of the day gradually increased, along with the insect chirps all around. People were stirring too. The Sun, he noted, had the power of light, warmth, and life.

Peter finished preparing his cameras, double-checked his settings, and then lowered himself into his chair, ready for the show to begin. The moment when the Moon first made contact with the Sun was blocked by a low, thin cloud hovering just above the horizon. With relief, the eclipsing Sun rose above it, and the whole sky above was clear. Peter knew then he had made the right choice to come inland to see the eclipse. He felt his shoulders relax as he breathed out, letting go of his frustrations from the previous night, along with any concerns about clouds.

Time to the total eclipse then transitioned very slowly. Peter talked to the people around him, and was surprised at how ill-prepared many of them were. Some had no camping equipment or protection from the harsh environment. Others did not even have solar filters and were unable to view the partial eclipse. He shared his glasses so others could enjoy the view. But he held back from fully engaging, as he wanted to remain focused during totality.

As the partial eclipse progressed, the temperature on his bare arms cooled. He shuddered, estimating the temperature had dropped around five degrees from the earlier heat of the morning.

The change in quality of light surprised Peter even more than the temperature drop. The light was now unlike anything he had ever experienced before. It was intense, focused, and sharp—while also appearing dull. He noted the richness of color in the earth around him, a deep red. The reduced light from the Sun painted the nearby landscape, with the colors fading from minute to minute.

Peter knew it would be difficult for his cameras to pick up all these subtle and unexpected changes. He closed his eyes to focus with clarity on the moment. A light breeze blew on his face, and he imagined Nature itself was breathing. Waiting. Whispering. Sharing news of an imminent arrival.

He returned to the task at hand, carefully watching the time. Minutes before totality, he removed his solar filter from his camera and made his final adjustments. He was ready. The light rapidly diminished, and he felt a huge wave of euphoria rush through him—just like he did during his tornado-chasing activities. The wind had stopped, creating a dramatic pause. He too stopped breathing as he awaited the imminent arrival of the Moon's shadow.

Peter heard the screams of others in the distance before the full shadow reached him. The darkness fell over the land, and the crowd cheered and clapped with excitement. Peter gasped as his forearms broke out in goosebumps. There it was: the beautiful diamond ring. And then totality.

It was how he imagined from the pictures he had seen, but so much more. It was all around him, and he trembled with a respectful fear. He tried to say something profound for his recording but couldn't quite find the words. All that came out were random noises. He simply stood there in reverence, in the darkness of the eclipsed Sun. It was like the Universe commanded his full attention, reaching into his soul and stripping back the layers of whom he was. He was but one person in a grand Universe. His heart was bursting with euphoria, and everything was all about that one moment.

After the cheers of excitement from the crowd came hushed and respectful silence. He recognized it was not just humans who were hushed into silence—nature seemed to stop too, like it had reset during totality. There was an eeriness to the silence in the presence of so many people.

The corona looked like the petals of a flower, emanating from the eclipsed Sun. It was the most beautiful and peaceful natural sight he had experienced, and soon it would be over. He did all he could to take it in, looking around him and trying to capture an image in his mind's eye. He was surprised to see similar colors as he had seen moments earlier during sunrise; but this time, the colors were low on the horizon all around him. Up above was dark. It didn't make sense. And then suddenly, the second diamond ring appeared. He watched as long as he could before the full brightness of the Sun returned.

Moments later, flocks of cockatoos ascended into the air, their horrendous screeching filling the valley with a harsh reality.

After feeling immersed in his own world with the Universe for that time, he returned to where he was. He saw others around him hugging, and some were even crying. For Peter, it was a moving and personal experience, which was deep, uplifting, and comforting. He didn't want to talk to others about what he had felt. But he was happy to celebrate the wonder they had all experienced together on the lookout. He turned to his neighbors and grinned as they high-fived each other.

It wasn't the isolated experience he had been looking for, but that didn't matter anymore. The crowds added an element to it all that he was not expecting. He was pretty happy with how things had turned out—tired, but happy.

Peter was certain of one thing: he was adding total eclipses to his list of nature obsessions.

III. TABITHA

The Reunion-Planner

TABITHA WOKE AT 4:00 A.M. She stretched out her arms in the dark, her fingers catching the mosquito net over her camp bed, and poked her head out of the tent. The stars shined brightly, and she heaved a sigh of relief. She quietly left her tent, avoiding the annoying zipping noises that are the usual soundtrack to camping. She could hear others starting to stir. She set about preparing the tea, a job she loved. Simon joined her and they commenced breakfast. Once everything was set, they all huddled together to welcome in the sunrise. They used their solar filters to see the sunrise, marveling at how unique an experience that was. Tabitha saw the Sun as a powerful life force, and could see it play out that morning with the dawn chorus of noise.

Tabitha saw a line of clouds on the horizon, but the rest of the sky was clear. She had done it—they would definitely see the eclipse! There was nothing else to do, except to watch and wait.

Just as they were starting the countdown to the eclipse, Tabitha realized she didn't actually know what to expect. But it was too late for that—it was starting! Through her filters, she saw it: a tiny outline of the edge of the Moon, there in front of the Sun. Tabitha gasped in wonder and also relief, reassured that things were happening as predicted.

The eclipse progressed much slower than expected, so Tabitha set about the task of making another round of tea for everyone. She took the occasional peek through her eclipse glasses and also glanced around to see how the light was changing. The family took turns explaining what they were seeing to her three-year-old niece. This seemed to give them a sense of control, despite not knowing what was to come.

As the eclipse progressed, the light dimmed and the colors faded. The light appeared as if they were under dimming halogen lights. They had, moments earlier, watched the sunrise, feeling the Sun's warmth penetrate the world around them. Now, it was like late afternoon with the light quickly dissipating. The natural order of the world seemed out of sync. Tabitha had a creeping sense of unease in the pit of her stomach, and she wasn't sure whether it was excitement or fear. The dimmer it got, the less they all spoke.

As Tabitha looked around the dry outback with a view of fields of crops, she suddenly thought of the horror film *Children of the Corn*. She recalled how the film featured a blue wash screen to transform day into night. And here, in a similar remote environment, the same light effect occurred. Everything was oddly silent, like all life was reaching a standstill. They were just like the birds—totally silent, flocked together in a group, and still. Despite the eeriness, Tabitha was not frightened. Instead, she found it both mesmerising and beautiful.

The suddenness of totality took Tabitha by surprise. She had no idea it would be as dramatic and intense, and she screamed out in surprise. She intuitively took her glasses off and saw the diamond ring, poignantly suspended in time. Then, as the final moments of light were gone, she couldn't quite believe what she saw. The Sun and the Moon had locked together, cast into full darkness.

Tabitha imagined herself as a Japanese animation cartoon character, with her hands to her head screaming. She couldn't quite believe she was in the real word, watching a real event. Their collective screams then turned to laughter at the absurdity of it all, which seemed to break the spell Tabitha was under. She could breathe again. As everyone retreated into their own experience, things went quiet.

The corona captivated Tabitha's full attention. She couldn't quite make sense of the silvery blue corona, which looked like a moving oil painting. She knew of no colors that could ever capture the majesty of what she was witnessing. The flames from the Sun reached right out toward her, like huge, friendly sunlight arms, ready to engulf her. The Sun wrapped its arms around her and touched her to the core, her soul. In a moment, a million words were said in no words.

Tabitha also felt a connection and sense of warmth to others around her—even strangers who were camping nearby. She didn't want to shift her gaze away from the splendor in front of her, but she could sense their presence and their awe. She wondered if others were also feeling the same physical presence she was.

She knew that totality was coming to an end, yet she didn't want to turn her eyes away. And then things shifted rapidly. She saw the second diamond ring as the shadow moved on. She heard shouts to put their glasses back on. Yet she kept looking—she didn't want to let it go. Simon nudged her, telling her to stop looking. She didn't want to miss a moment of what was happening, but she reluctantly turned her gaze away. It was over. She could still see tiny diamond rings when she blinked for some time. She stood momentarily in stunned silence, as the normal world again came back.

They all hugged, trying to find the words to share their experiences. Together they questioned whether they did in fact witness the implausible. Did that really happen? Or was it just a CGI effect that someone had planned? Did they imagine it all? But she knew it was real. She could still feel the embrace of totality. And she felt older, wiser.

Tabitha remained glued to the spot, keeping the Moon company as it continued its journey across the Sun. The others returned to their seats around their camp, talking excitedly. Yet she wanted to give her full adoration and respect to the Moon, for what it had given her. She watched until the Moon finally was no longer visible and the eclipse was over.

Tabitha then returned to her family, feeling like she saw things in a different way through new eyes. Her sister handed her a cup of tea. Their very special family moment had arrived, and it was even more amazing than they ever expected it to be. Every one of them felt deeply affected in some way. Now, instead of the eclipse of 2012 being a future focal point for them all, it was a memory. The future was now wide open with possibilities.

IV. SIMON

The Backpacker

SIMON WOKE NATURALLY IN THE early morning. He didn't quite know what time it was, but he was aware that others in their camp, and beyond, were stirring. He lay back with his eyes open, thinking about where he was and where he had come.

Also in his thoughts were all the nature experiences he had had over the last two years in Australia. *This is a very special country,* he thought, and he knew that at some point he would be moving on. But for the present time, on this day, he was glad to be here.

He heard movement nearby and noticed Tabitha leaving her tent. He stumbled out of his sleeping bag and joined her to help prepare tea and breakfast for everyone. She had been carrying the angst for all of them, and he was glad to see her relax a little. He figured the clear sky had a lot to do with it. He was content with whatever was to happen.

Pretty soon everyone came together for breakfast. He had watched many a sunrise, but this was the first time he watched the sunrise with solar filters. It was like he was seeing the Sun as a round star for the first time, and was impressed that the ball of orange in the sky was their Sun, powerful and ever-present.

He smiled as he compared this view to his first eclipse back in 1999. Back then, there were thick clouds in the sky and he was in party mode. This time, he was a decade older and in a much better state to appreciate the eclipse.

Through the glasses he was able to spot that moment of first contact, when the Moon was first visible over the Sun. It was both reassuring and amazing that these moments could be predicted with such accuracy. The following stages of the partial eclipse occurred slower than he expected.

As the partial eclipse progressed, Simon thought it looked a little like Pac-Man. He also saw and felt a change in the environment. He couldn't quite figure out what was unsettling about it. He struggled to identify the emotions he felt, unlike any feeling he had experienced before. The logical part of his brain knew what was to happen—

informed from what he had read and experienced before. But another part of him felt an eerie fear—that something big and unexpected was going down. Simon had never felt that sense before, as if it were deeper than words, or deeper than what he was seeing. It was like he knew what was approaching, but *didn't* know. There was an energy to his surroundings, as if he were entering a new, unknown world.

Simon noted that it seemed like the day was now in reverse. Earlier, they watched the day break, with the Sun beating down on them. Now here they were, moments later, and light was dimming. The light changed quickly, and he was aware of the absence of birds, an odd, unnatural experience. The light coming from the Sun was now like a beam, getting thinner and thinner. And then, dramatically, the darkness descended and the world changed. Totality had arrived, and it felt powerful and intense. Waves of excitement and energy coursed through his body, and he struggled to contain it all. Simon didn't know quite what to do with himself, and he found himself screaming, and then dancing.

Simon knew that totality would be a special experience. But he had not expected things to be this intense. He knew instinctively that he could now view totality without filters and couldn't quite believe what he was seeing. All he could manage was to say, "Whoaaaa." There above him, suspended in the sky, was the eclipsed Sun. Totality. Mesmerized by the beauty of totality, he fell silent.

He noticed a blue light emanating from behind the Moon, which he knew was the corona. But he also noticed wonder all around him too. He wanted to look in every direction at once. He tore his eyes away and took in the eeriness of colors in the landscape around him. He never knew colors like that existed in the natural world. *Magical* was the best word—he felt that captured it, as it was unique, special, and inexplicable. He hadn't seen anything quite like it in all of his travels so far. He was meant to be there, at that moment in time, and he knew he would remember this for life.

Everyone was transfixed, taking as much in as they could. Something special was happening to everyone who was experiencing totality. He felt connected with the Universe, the planets above, and some sort of energy. Unexpectedly, his mother's presence filled his soul, and he was comforted in a way he hadn't felt for a long time.

He saw the start of the second diamond ring and knew it was over. He couldn't quite believe how beautiful, amazing, and wondrous totality was. He felt full of love and joy. Turning to Tabitha, he saw that she was still looking, even as the light was rapidly returning. He yelled at her, and then nudged her urgently to get her glasses on. He was not one to follow rules in life, but he understood the need for filters when the Sun returned.

After they hugged and celebrated, Simon wanted to continue sharing with others. He couldn't quite find the right words, but it didn't matter—they had just shared this life-changing event. He left Tabitha to watch the remaining partial eclipse and joined the rest of the family. The rules of nature were restored, and life had returned back to normal. Yet something had changed. He reflected upon moments and memories from the past that he was not expecting, and he felt at peace.

V. TERRY

The Festival-Goer

TERRY AWOKE AT AROUND 5:00 a.m. and stumbled out of his tent into the semidarkness. It took him a little time to orient himself. He tread carefully through the tangle of tents—some with people still in them—toward the main stage. Music was playing, and revelers were still dancing even at this hour. These were the ones who wanted to stay up and greet the eclipse. He followed the zombie-like crowd, moving now as one, beyond the main stage and toward the ridge. He was awestruck at the hundreds—perhaps thousands—of people already there, using light from torches and mobile phones to move around. He shuddered, excited to be a part of this special occasion.

Knowing it was pointless to find his friends in such a large crowd, he found a spot on his own and settled in. He did what he needed to do to prepare for this celestial alignment. He wondered what state his friends were in, having stayed up all night. He sure hoped they didn't miss it.

It was some time since Terry had mindfully watched a sunrise. The orange and purple colors seemed almost dreamlike from his vantage point. It was a vibrant experience that he made a mental note to repeat. The sky was clear, apart from a low bank of light cloud that was hanging around just above the horizon, but it wasn't enough to block the Sun. He smiled at his luck, wondering how his family fared with the clouds back down along the coast.

As the Sun rose, the birds greeted the day with their early-morning commotion of sound. Terry soon became uncomfortably warm and he realized it was only going to get much worse being so exposed with no shade. There would be no returning to the main stage to cool off while this show was going on. He wiped the sweat off his forehead with the back of his hand, and put on his hat.

Through his filters, Terry saw a tiny imperfection on the top left edge of the Sun—was that the Moon? A few moments later, the crowd noticed too, and cheered and whistled as the eclipse started. The crowd noises then settled back down to a background chatter. Terry felt crowds were like flocks of birds, or even waves, with sounds rising and falling. The size of the crowd together, all watching the same thing, was so powerful.

He listened in to the conversations and comments around him. People shouted out, "Go, Moon!" as if it needed encouragement to do its thing. Others were coming out with witty one-liners that he would never have thought of, which made him break out in a wide smile. Many commented about the partially eclipsed Sun looking like Pac-Man. It *did* look like Pac-Man. The mood was jovial and lighthearted. At one point, a small group started singing "Happy Birthday" to Kieran, and this then traveled around to the larger group, with others joining in. *Lucky Kieran,* Terry thought. Imagine having the Universe mark the occasion of one's birthday with this. Although alone, Terry did not feel alone. He felt part of the crowd sitting on the ridge, all coming together for the same purpose.

The Moon continued to move in front of the Sun, now well over 50 percent covered. The crowd became more subdued, with most sitting quietly, mirroring the silence of nature.

He sighed in relief when the temperature started to drop—when around 90 percent of the Sun was covered. The wind had picked up too, giving him a bit of a reprieve from the heat. In fact, he felt a little chill after sweating earlier. The chill was also from the darkening sky. There seemed to be a feeling of something building, like a storm about to break.

Terry noticed the Moon's shadow coming in from the west, like a creeping darkness. Then, before he knew it, the darkness descended upon them and the Sun suddenly went out. He leaped up, the sudden build-up now too intense. He cried out unknowingly, joining with the screams of excitement of everyone around him. Looking through his solar filters, he could no longer see any sign of the Sun at all—just pure darkness. He then knew it was safe. The Sun was gone, and he could look at totality directly. He threw his hat to the ground to get a better view. It looked like a black hole in the sky, and was much bigger than he was expecting. It was a weird feeling, which sent chills down his spine.

He saw a black circle, with white light that faded into what seemed like a helix coming from behind the darkness. It was like a wormhole, but with outer rays shining around the edges. There were shapes and colors—a silvery blue— that he was not expecting. His thoughts then turned to what a black hole consuming the Earth would look like, and he supposed it would look something like this. Terry thought it was the coolest thing he had ever seen.

He then noticed the stars above. He spotted what he thought was Venus and a few bright stars.

The initial crowd euphoria had passed, and it was now eerily silent. Everyone was in full respect of the Universe. He shuddered in the cool atmosphere, surprised that he could be feeling quite cold. He lost track of time—staring for what could have been minutes, or even hours.

Terry was not ready for the sudden return of the light. Another wave of euphoria hit, and then totality was over. Along with the light, the volume of the world increased, with a return to natural noise. The crowd around him cheered, clapped, and hugged; but Terry just wanted the eclipse to come back.

People started to move away, still hugging and clearly energized and up for partying. But Terry wanted to stay to watch the rest of the eclipse. There was still much more of the partial eclipse to go, and he was enjoying the ride.

Terry stayed and watched the whole eclipse until he could no longer see any of the Moon when viewed through his eclipse glasses. It was over. The Sun was back with a vengeance. It felt much hotter again, and he was now dripping with sweat. Despite his discomfort, he felt a new respect for the energy of the nearest star.

He climbed down from the ridge and made his way back to the main stage area, cooling off under the stage sprinklers. The water seemed to mark a physical transition back to festival life again. The energy of the crowd was almost palpable, and he was ready to celebrate the momentous celestial alignment. As he joined the massive crowd on the main dance area, his mind wandered back to the eclipse and the shapes and colors he had seen. It was out of this world. He felt out of this world, united as one with the other dancers.

After a while, Terry wandered back to see his artist friends. One of his mates had gotten too drunk and slept through the whole show. Once he woke up, his friend shrugged and said he hadn't wanted to see the eclipse anyway.

VI. ROSE

The Wishful Teacher

ROSE SET HER OWN ALARM at 4:00 a.m. She sprang up when it went off and ran outside in the darkness—in her pajamas—eager to see if the weather was clear. She saw stars up above and did a little happy dance on the spot. There were clouds about, but she hoped they would stay away on this special morning.

With the radio on, she got ready for their little family gathering and waited until 5:00 a.m. before waking up her son. She was expecting this to be a bit of a battle, as he would always plead for ten more minutes. Instead, he woke straight away and bounced out of bed, shouting, "It's eclipse day!" Seeing him so thrilled about the eclipse fed into her excitement even more. They both tried to contain the sounds of their excitement as they made their way down the street toward her mother's house. Other houses had lights on too, preparing to welcome in the sunrise on this special day.

On arrival, her son joined his father on the balcony while Rose worked with her mother to put together their special eclipse breakfast. She smiled at her mother, listening to the excited chatter of her son. Being together as a family on this special day felt right.

With the morning light came even more clouds, which prevented them from seeing the start of the eclipse. But there were moments when the clouds thinned and they caught glimpses of the partially eclipsed Sun through their glasses. They clapped whenever the clouds thinned to give them a view. Through their filters, the eclipsed Sun was a deep orange with a bite taken out. The Sun was much larger than she had expected. This is how the world should be—this moment had been precisely predicted.

Rose kept an eye on the time, ensuring that they were aware of when the key moments were to happen. With around ten minutes to go before totality, the light had dimmed and everything appeared gray and washed out.

Then, with the strangest timing, her mother announced she was going to take a shower and her ex-partner announced he would go inside to make another round of coffee. Gasping, Rose insisted that no one was leaving. They were to stay there and watch. She wanted to make sure they were all together, and that no one missed a thing.

She then noticed something odd. Earlier, they had the full brightness of the morning Sun—even behind the cloud. But now, it seemed a little eerie. The air felt dark and heavy, like before a storm. They all stood up to take it in, feeling a slight breeze. She shuddered.

The darkness descended, and the Moon's shadow had arrived. She wasn't sure, but she felt it was okay to look without their glasses. Rose noticed that it was quite dark, darker than she had expected. Then the miraculous happened: the clouds parted, and she could see the fully eclipsed Sun. It took her breath away. She couldn't believe what she was seeing. Beside her, her son was jumping up and down, screaming out, "It's awesome! It's amazing!"

Totality captivated Rose. She found herself repeating, "I can't believe it." Not only was it an incredible sight, but it also filled her with an intensely good feeling. Like a warm joy spreading from the top of her head to the tips of her toes. It was like nothing else in the world should be happening in those moments—only totality. The rest of the world no longer existed. Time had stopped, and those two minutes felt like a lifetime.

She thought it was the most awe-inspiring thing that we could ever experience. She tried to take a few photos of totality, while trying to watch it, and didn't do a great job of either.

She had a profound thought: totality was not just about her. It was about the whole Universe, solar system and beyond. She was in no way prepared to have such an immersive event or such deep thoughts. Rose couldn't recall a time when everyone in a whole region stopped what they were doing and looked up. She could almost sense everyone being as awestruck as she was, right at that moment.

The clouds were still parted, and Rose looked around and up at the sky, spotting Venus. She then noticed things changing again and sensed that totality was coming to an end. The euphoria returned as she screamed out. She saw the final diamond ring at the end, understanding why it had that name. And then, the light returned dramatically. It was over. She hurriedly shouted at everyone to put their glasses back on.

Totality was over, and she desperately missed it. She now understood the pull that eclipse chasers felt to chase eclipses all around the world. She hoped that she could too one day. Her heart was full of pride and contentment to have seen this eclipse with her family, making the occasion special for her son. She was quite sure he would remember it for the rest of his life. She knew she would.

They continued to watch the partial eclipse, looking through their glasses. The cloud still remained parted, giving them more of a view than what they had earlier when the eclipse first started. But soon, clouds covered the partially eclipsed Sun. Rose knew the best of it was over. With a deep, satisfied sigh, she turned to her mother and told her that it was now a good time to take a shower.

3

READJUSTING
TO THE LIGHT

CHAPTER 5

RETURN TO NORMALITY

I. CARA

The Newlywed

ONCE THE ECLIPSE WAS OVER, Cara sat in the camper with the door wide open, fanning herself to cool down. Mike sidled over beside her, and together they looked through the photos he had taken. She couldn't believe it had gotten so dark.

They discussed Mike's freak-out moment during totality and wondered how he could have gotten so confused. He was frustrated that his uncertainty ate into precious moments of totality.

Cara still shook from the experience, slightly unsettled. What exactly was normal, now that she had seen the impossible? She desperately wanted to experience totality again, to try to make sense of it. She wanted to talk to others. Was anyone else feeling confused?

She turned on the radio and listened to the live broadcast from their original location outside of Mareeba. The radio announcer was talking incoherently with intensity. It didn't matter—she could relate to the confusion and it seemed to help her understand that others felt just like she did.

There were cuts to interviews with different people, and all were saying the same thing. The total eclipse experience was amazing and indescribable, and they now understood what the fuss was all about. There was a sense of unity conveyed in the broadcasts—locals and tourists said the same thing and felt connected.

Cara made an interesting observation: the locals were well known for being pragmatic. Yet here, some talked about their emotions and feelings of connections. Many choked up as they tried to express profound new insights. Listening to the replay of totality gave Cara goosebumps, especially when the crowd screamed as the shadow arrived. How lucky she was to have chosen this region out of all regions, at the right time to experience this! She now felt very much a part of her new community through this shared experience. She then heard my voice on the radio—as incoherent as the other interviewees, which she found reassuring. She knew it was all going to be okay.

As much as they would have loved to stay on for a few days, it was time to go, as Mike had to return to work. Oh, to be on holidays like the international eclipse chasers! They packed up and calling Yoda in, they drove down the narrow dirt track back onto the Mulligan Highway, joining the exodus heading south. They saw even more vehicles and camps along the side of the road. Despite the heavy traffic, it flowed well and there was a friendly feel. Everyone waved and tooted their horns. Never before had she been part of such a large, shared experience on such an epic scale.

A few hours later, they turned into their driveway on the farm. They had only been away for one night, but Cara returned home as a different person. Mike then said his goodbyes and left for work, leaving Cara alone with Yoda and her memories of the eclipse.

Cara phoned her family and friends to share what they had experienced. She struggled to find the words to communicate how special it was, in a way they could fully appreciate. She tried different ways to describe what she saw, but they were not understanding the immensity of it all. She gave up and said her goodbyes. She wondered if she could ever communicate what had just happened, how she had changed. And now, she felt a dip in her energy. The eclipse was over, the excitement was over, and now it was as if there was a large gap in her life. Mike called her from work, explaining that everyone at his work had "post-eclipse depression." Others were feeling this dip too.

For the rest of the day, Cara continued to listen to the local radio, still focused on the eclipse. She wondered how the schedules would be filled now that the eclipse was over; it had been the focus for so long. Cara was in no way ready for the world to move on. She wanted to stay with the excited build-up that had been happening for weeks and certainly didn't want to let go of those euphoric moments of totality.

The next day, she went into Mareeba and found it full of tourists and locals, still buzzing about the eclipse. Cara swelled with pride at having the town in the international spotlight. Every new encounter started the same way: "Did you see it?" But as the days went on, the crowds reduced and life returned to normal. The eclipse was yesterday's news. Cara felt a huge gap where the eclipse had been.

In the weeks following the eclipse, Cara thought about seeing the eclipse again and about their future plans. She felt energized and eager to explore options for the future.

Weeks later, looking back at newspaper reports, it dawned on Cara that the darkness they experienced was the Moon's shadow. Of course, she had heard this before in news reports, but she suddenly realized the immensity of this. Her clearest visual memory was of how quickly the darkness descended, and that she could see some stars during the day. Importantly, she did not forget one moment of how she *felt*. For her, that ominous feeling of impending doom, followed by the most euphoric moment of her life, was as strong as if she had experienced totality yesterday. She got goosebumps just thinking about it.

II. PETER

The Storm-Chaser

AFTER THE FINAL PART OF the eclipse was over, Peter packed up his belongings. He had a six-hour drive south to get to work and was eager to get going before traffic became a problem.

As he drove, Peter estimated there were up to a thousand vehicles parked bumper to bumper along the side of the road leading up to the Lookout. It was an unusual sight in such a rural outback landscape. The traffic thickened as he drove—much heavier than the day before on his drive up. But thankfully, it flowed well.

During his rest stops, friendly people shared their stories and experiences about the eclipse. One man knew a lady who had told him that she wasn't going to wake up early to see the eclipse. She had said, "Oh, I've seen hundreds of these before—they happen all the time." He found it difficult to understand how someone could be so closed off to experiencing something new. Especially now that he knew how profound an experience it was.

When he arrived back in Townsville, Peter was eager to talk to everyone about what they saw. Everyone reported it was amazing and commented on how dark it got—yet they were not within the path of totality. They had not experienced any of the features he had seen by driving hours north to get into the path. They did not know, nor seem to understand, that there was so much more to the experience. He found it difficult to describe the subtle details—the quality of the light; the richness of the colors; the drop in temperature. Words could not convey the immensity of these visceral experiences to others. He also had no words to explain how magnificent totality was, and what they had missed. His video footage also failed to convey the eeriness of it all. He realized that you just had to experience totality yourself to fully understand it.

Peter yearned to experience totality again. He was surprised that he felt so alone, as no one else nearby had experienced the immensity of what he had experienced. He wanted to find his tribe—to share his experiences with eclipse chasers, so he could make sense of it without the frustration of describing something outside of normal experience, that no one nearby had even seen.

III. TABITHA

The Reunion-Planner

TABITHA HADN'T KNOWN WHAT TO expect with the eclipse, but totality exceeded her expectations. She had watched the sunrise, and then there was a morning, dusk, twilight, darkness, dawn, and then a return to the day. The movie *Twilight Zone* best captured the incomprehensibility of it all. How wonderful that the world is full of surprises!

After packing up their camp and saying goodbye to the rest of the family, Tabitha and Simon drove the thirty minutes or so to the Eclipse Festival. The energy was electric, as if the eclipse had charged the crowd with an incredible power. She wondered what totality would have been like in such a crowd of like-minded people. Laughing, she realized she would just have to see another total eclipse to find out. However, her intimate family experience was perfect. She wouldn't have changed anything.

In the days following the eclipse, Tabitha and Simon together enjoyed their holiday in the region, before they returned back to their respective lives. Tabitha found herself thinking a lot about her totality experience, trying to make sense of it. She pictured that something happened to her soul, something that made her feel so much more confident about her life. She walked taller and felt more centered and wiser, as if she had strengthened as a person.

Growing up, the eclipse had been a significant marker in Tabitha's life, a stable focal point that helped her to move forward. She felt closure when she saw the next full Moon. She recognized this was the same Moon that had filled her with such a beautiful experience just weeks ago. Fondly, she said goodbye to that Moon. It was time to write a new chapter in the book of her life.

IV. SIMON

The Backpacker

IT TOOK SIMON QUITE A while to feel grounded after totality; the experience shook him. He had known that the total eclipse would be a meaningful event, but he had not expected it to be so personal, so moving, and to touch his core in the way that it had. His thoughts were on his mother—he longed for her. Yet he was comforted by her presence during totality, as if she were there and all around him. The experience raised many questions about the world and what life was all about. He felt a new sense of clarity and purpose, with a dash of puzzlement.

He talked through what he had seen and experienced with Tabitha's family, and also with the older couple who had "intruded" on their campsite. They would all be lifelong friends now, having shared something so intense and meaningful.

He wanted to celebrate the eclipse and figured that the Eclipse Festival down the road would be a great place to visit. He had the buzz of the Universe in him! He was eager to connect with others about their experience, wanting to learn what others felt and how they were making sense of the experience. He also wanted to sit with those more challenging feelings of uncertainty about what life was all about. Life was mysterious, and it was okay not to have all the answers.

Over the following week, the eclipse experience was at the forefront of his mind. Camping under the stars, swimming in volcanic lakes, swimming in rainforest creeks—there was a magical quality to the land. It was like the eclipse opened up another channel to fully appreciate the natural beauty of the region. He wanted to drink in every moment of this unique place while he could.

He was aware that he was arriving to a new insight, as if the eclipse had highlighted an important direction. He looked at life differently, motivated to make a few changes. These things floated around in his mind before the eclipse, but now everything seemed much clearer. He wanted to look after himself more, so he would be around for longer, so he could enjoy more in life.

There was an interesting circle of completion following this eclipse. His partying ways started in 1999 at the Eclipse Festival in England and it ended with another eclipse, and another Eclipse Festival. The circle of his early adult life felt complete.

V. TERRY

The Festival-Goer

THE REST OF ECLIPSE DAY was epic. Terry danced with a vigorous intensity as the good vibes flowed, the crowd moving as one. The music sounded out of this world, as if they were broadcasting to the cosmos. This was a party like no other, to celebrate their brief encounter with the inner workings of the Universe.

As the day wore on, the energy drained and Terry needed to physically replenish. Walking back to his tent for a rest, he saw some were leaving the festival. He was curious about this. Perhaps the environment was a little too extreme? Or maybe the eclipse was the peak moment for them. For him, he was still very much up for partying, and the festival was not over. He wanted to share the vibe of the eclipse with those who remained. The energy was different in the final days—gone was the feeling of build-up. Instead, it was a shared feeling of joy and happiness. On the final day (two days after the eclipse), he said goodbye to his newfound friends. He packed up his gear, and then returned back to his normal life back in his home at Clifton Beach.

He was eager to talk to his family about their eclipse experience in much more detail. He soon learned that many who remained on the coast had issues with clouds during totality. In fact, more people missed the eclipse than saw it. His mother watched from their home balcony, standing on a chair to see over the nature reserve with trees. Despite the clouds and obstructed view, she enjoyed the experience. His father was away, and had watched from a live feed but wishing he were there. Terry felt very lucky that he had experienced the eclipse at the festival, with such clear skies; though he was a little sad for those who missed out. He struggled to share how amazing it was from the festival, and felt he couldn't go on about it when so many people missed it.

He returned to work, listening to the stories of others and how intense it was with the clouds threatening to cover the main show. Over time, he kept quiet about his own experiences, not wanting to make them feel jealous. He knew deep down he was incredibly lucky. The whole festival experience, with the eclipse, was one of the most intense and profound moments of his life.

VI. ROSE

The Wishful Teacher

ROSE MADE IT TO WORK on time. Everyone wanted to share what had happened. "Did you see it?" was the main question; and of course, many hadn't because of the cloud cover. Rose realized she was very lucky that, at her location, the clouds had parted during totality. She had a great discussion within her own class, asking the children how they saw it, and took the time to allow everyone to share their stories. She was a little dismayed, though, when she asked a class later in the day and the response was, "Miss, that was this morning." She wasn't ready to move on!

After school, she was able to watch the recording of the breakfast TV show that featured the whole eclipse live from Palm Cove. She saw the clouds had parted there too at the most crucial moment, and everyone experienced totality, as she had done. She watched the recording over and over again, getting goosebumps as the crowd screamed with excitement when the shadow arrived. It was thrilling being able to see it from a new perspective, in a different location.

She spoke to a friend living outside of the path of totality, who was frustrated that the whole morning TV show had been focused on the total eclipse. Her friend could not see why it was so special. Rose found it difficult to communicate the intensity and uniqueness of the experience. She may as well have been speaking Japanese.

In the mornings following the eclipse, Rose found herself waking up with lots of energy at 5:00 a.m.—very different to her usual way of life. She loved the buzz and energy. She wanted to take on the world.

Life returned to normal—the eclipse tourists had left and the eclipse was no longer the first topic of conversation. So many others had a cloudy experience and did not feel the intensity like she had, so she felt quite isolated in her experience. She wasn't ready to return to normal; she didn't *feel* normal. She wanted to see it again. She wanted to keep talking about it—to people who knew and understood. She wanted those intense feelings of being alive to stay with her. She spent hours every evening looking up news reports, videos, and images of the eclipse. She also sought out astronomy sites—something she had not done in the past.

After a week, Rose felt her energy drop, as if she were coming off a natural buzz. There was emptiness. The excitement of the build-up was gone and the eclipse was over. News was just news again, and there was nothing to look forward to. She had to adjust to fitting into her old way of life, when she desperately wanted to find a new way.

She knew that the next eclipse in the region was in two hundred years. Her only option to see another eclipse was to travel—to become an eclipse chaser. But her life circumstances, for the next few years at least, would limit her freedom to do so.

CHAPTER 6

ECLIPSE INSIGHTS

The total eclipse experience is greatly influenced by past events, personal beliefs, and life circumstances. In this chapter, we will explore how each of the beings in the shadow made sense of the eclipse experience. That is, how the experience made them think about their lives, the insights they gained, and what they thought of the eclipse. Interviews have been sensitively edited and restructured to provide a cohesive overview, but remain each individual's own words.

I. CARA

The Newlywed

I DIDN'T ANTICIPATE BEING DRAWN into the total eclipse. I like to go to a particular natural occurrence, whether it be a volcano or a waterfall, or trees growing around ancient civilizations, ruins—things like that. When you travel to see something natural, you are just a person on a holiday seeing this thing that is always there. But an eclipse is different. I would never have sought the experience out. I would have seen it on the news and just would have said, "Oh yeah, whatever." I'm really glad we had coincidently moved here when it happened, because I wouldn't have seen it otherwise.

The eclipse is definitely something I am now interested in. What I didn't realize was how great the build-up is. There is this feeling of anticipation with everyone around you. It was exciting.

Mike and I have been really proactive in the time since the eclipse and definitely have a buzz about us. The eclipse was a wake-up call about what we are doing and what is important.

During totality, it was dark, like a navy-blue darkness. I was surprised at how scary that ring looked to me, and how I felt an ominous feeling, like impending doom, or something like that. I was looking at it thinking, *Oh, this isn't good. That's not right.*

I was surprised at how quickly the stars came out, and that they came out at all. I had this thought: *What if you didn't know this was about to happen?* That's what I found so scary about the eclipse. Totality reinforced a feeling that despite our attempts to create order, we are not really in control.

I have been thinking about how similar that feeling was to the Brisbane floods in 2011. I was in one of the most affected areas of the city. We were evacuated. We had no electricity for five days. We were all walking around the streets with garbage bags and trolleys, moving things for each other and helping each other out. After that, you learn that you are not in control of the environment. We are just these insignificant participants at the whim of the river and the river is going to do what the river wants to do. I felt that way after totality, because the most basic thing you can trust—that the Sun will come up and the Sun will go down—was challenged. You think you know—there will be day, then night. The total eclipse challenged that basic premise.

It reminded me of mortality, in the sense that these are the conditions we require and the Sun is our life force. And the Sun was gone. There is all this stuff happening out there, and we are just these little specks looking up at this thing going in front of this other thing that provides everything we need. I was so amazed at how bright the light was, even from a tiny sliver of the Sun. How huge and bright it must be!

At the time, I felt like I had seen the impossible. I'm a little less thrown by it now, I guess. Now I just think it was a great experience. I'd love to do it again and so would Mike. Now that he knows he can look at it.

I felt a connection to all the people I had seen down the dirt road, and to all the people who had sought out that experience. The sense of togetherness, and the feeling that only we who experienced it could fully appreciate what had transpired was very special.

I'd like to chase another eclipse, to see totality again. I'd also like to feel that wave again, that build-up, within the community.

Every year, my two best friends and I go away on holiday together. One lives in Darwin, and the other in Melbourne, so it is hard for us to see each other. The friend in Darwin saw the partial eclipse. I asked her if she wanted to go to the next eclipse, and she thought it was a great idea. Traveling to another eclipse together would be a great way to see each other.

Either I might go with the girls for our once-a-year trip, or Mike and I will do something together. It's great to have an adventure to take us completely away from what we are doing. I have been researching the next eclipse or two. I wouldn't want to pay a hefty sum for a tour, but if we could figure out a place where we could get to it on our own, then I'd love to.

I don't think I need all the details right now, though. I don't need to have this anxiety about how we could afford to chase it!

II. PETER

The Storm-Chaser

THE TOTAL ECLIPSE WAS INCREDIBLE. It took me to another level, a spiritual level I suppose you would call it. Where you connect with life, the Universe, and everything. It has been life-changing.

It was like I walked into a room and didn't really know what I was going to find behind that door. I went in completely unknowing. Before I experienced the total eclipse, I was like everyone else who had never seen one. You see it on TV, and you read things. I had seen the photos and videos. But until you experience it and feel it, it's impossible to know.

After you experience the eclipse, maybe it does create this other level of awareness. It's like opening a door—you are now opened to another experience you hope to have again and again. I'm not really religious. I feel I have nature in my soul. Since totality, however, I'm feeling this universal connection—it is like an energy.

It was really important to just be there, and the way things lined up to get me there was interesting. It just felt right. Everything was right with the world at that point.

I had a similar feeling when the very first tornado I ever saw formed over our heads. I got to experience a pretty rare thing. They call it the cinnamon swirl, where you can see right up into the developing tube of the tornado. There were no words; you are there just gasping with your mouth open. It was like that during totality. I was transfixed on that moment in place and time. Nothing outside that moment penetrates.

There is a difference between the eclipse and the storm-chasing. With the eclipse, you just have to mark it on the map. Obviously, you hope the weather is good, and you stand there and let it happen. In storm-chasing, there is a chase. There is more skill and luck involved.

I think you can connect these experiences back to nature. The eclipse, tornado-chasing, and severe weather: they are all interesting and intense nature experiences. They are *opening* experiences. Every time I go and experience these events, in as much as it is an outside experience, it makes you look inwardly. It makes you really assess your life—to look at where you are and what you want to do.

What I am overwhelmed with is the connection to others. People from around the world came together in the same geographical location. Like at Bob's Lookout: I thought I was going to view it on my own, but thousands of people turned up! What draws these people so strongly? It's a powerful thing, the eclipse.

A word—*convergence*—kind of makes sense. People are coming together to experience the same thing; there is a common thread. Mostly large convergences of people are due to man-made events: concerts, sports, that sort of thing. But with the eclipse, it's an external force—the Sun and the Moon are causing this to happen.

You end up connecting with other people who have had, or want to have, the totality experience. You have found your tribe. I would like to experience a total eclipse again, especially with people who understand the experience.

You hear about the Egyptians or the Mayans, those societies that were able to plot the stars in the sky. At some point, we have lost that link with these ancient cultures that already understood it. Indigenous people are more connected. Also, animals have a connection with nature. For example, you hear of horses knowing an earthquake is coming. I feel we are losing our connection to nature; we are shutting ourselves off from the natural world. The eclipse brings that connection back.

It really makes you think there is only a small percentage of our brain we use. Is it during these events that maybe some of those other portions of your brain turn on or synapses start communicating in a different way? It's really interesting to know whether you are having a human and chemical feeling, or if what is happening is more on an energy level. It's really hard to explain!

It could be a similar thing to someone who does take illicit drugs as part of their lifestyle. We are possibly doing the same thing with nature highs, in that our brain gets stimulated when the event happens. It's a natural way of doing it—nature is stimulating natural endorphins. That can't be a bad thing.

I'll be storm-chasing for the rest of my life. It's like a drug addiction—you feel bad when you are not getting that hit. Unfortunately, I might have got a bit of an addiction to the eclipse bug now too.

I definitely want to do it again, for sure. I tried to stop looking at when eclipses are going to happen, because I'm not sure I have the finances to do it. Seeing this total eclipse creates the frustration of not having the resources in life to experience it again. If I'm ignorant of the fact of where it's going to happen, then it's easier. At the moment, I really cannot afford to take on another natural addiction.

It's really interesting how the eclipse has made me reassess everything again. I've just put it down to the meaning of life, basically. It's the people around you, the people you meet, and the experiences you have. And that's basically it. If your funeral is tomorrow, I don't think anyone is going to say you were great because you have lots of material possessions. You are remembered for the life you live. And you should *really* live. The total eclipse has been a key life experience. I guess in my eulogy, I would want it to be in there for sure.

III. TABITHA

The Reunion-Planner

I WAS QUITE STRESSED OUT about the eclipse, about making it great, and the weather. I was a bit snappy and stressed out. Mom was kind of just laughing, but at the same time, she was like, *Wow, you are really stressed out.*

The total eclipse was a pinnacle moment in my life, especially because I had been leading up to it for so long. When the eclipse actually happened, it surpassed all expectations of what it would be. And that was the thing. I didn't know what it was going to be like. I had no idea, and had never seen one before. Nothing prepared me for what it actually was, physically, and the way it looked. That's why I screamed out so much. I had no idea.

The biggest thing for me was the corona and how the tendrils just gave this beautiful and lovely, huggy, warm, three-dimensional embrace. It was eerie. When I say *eerie,* I mean really beautiful and mysterious. It was a physical thing—it actually reached around me on the other side, like I was being held by something. Totality definitely touched my core, my soul. It felt awe-inspiring and comforting. It made me feel that everything is okay and there is nothing to worry about in this world. I don't have to get caught up in everything, no need to run in circles. Everything matters, but nothing matters. There is a picture in my mind that my experience of totality has done something to my soul, my being, that has made me feel really confident. I'm a confident person, anyway, but I do have some doubts, as we all do. It reached out and hugged me. I guess the experience has helped me grow up a little bit as well, from that feeling of worry and stress.

On a physical level, it was a whole new experience. In a way, it reaffirmed my purpose in life, and I suppose, the Universe.

My family has always given personality to the Moon and the Sun—I guess pagan-style worship. The Moon is a being, and the Sun gives life. During the eclipse, it was like the Sun and Moon were playful. It was like seeing a personality of the whole Universe, a glimpse of the essence of the Universe. Totality, with the Sun and the Moon together, had some kind of presence itself—a beautiful, happy light. It gave off this beautiful energy. It was beautiful and profound. It felt like the spirit of everything, and definitely a union. I wouldn't say it felt like a new being, it just seemed . . . maybe it was. It just felt like when totality happened, some portal opened up, allowing me to see the real Universe. This is quite hard to explain in words, isn't it? I guess the world is a mirror, and how you see things is a reflection of you. I feel like the whole Universe is inside you, and it's also out there.

I actually feel really positive. I had always thought that for the time of the eclipse, I should be doing the things I really wanted to be doing. And I am. The eclipse always helped me make the right decisions, even before I saw it.

I intend to live my life without being stagnant and want to do the things I really enjoy. Now that the eclipse is over, I'm actually really looking forward to the rest of life. It feels good. I feel like I have got a lot of creative inspiration from the experience and I can focus on that. It will probably send stuff in some other way, maybe in my dreams. I will definitely write songs about it.

I haven't experienced anything else like it in my life so it has to be a ten out of ten for impact on me. It hasn't changed me as a person, but it feels like it has confirmed everything I knew. It has reaffirmed everything I believe.

I was an eclipse chaser before—this was the one I was chasing. I'd love to see another one, and I am sure I will one day. I am very satisfied with that experience, but I'd love to experience another one.

IV. SIMON

The Backpacker

THE TOTAL ECLIPSE WAS AS good as I dreamed it was going to be. I knew it would be unique, but nothing prepares you for how special it is. When totality happens, it's unreal. I was trying to explain it afterward, but I was just lost for words. I didn't know what to do when it was happening. I was dancing, I was screaming—it was wild.

When totality starts, there is a feeling inside you, deep down, that something is going on. It's deeper than sight, it's deeper than words, and it's just a special feeling. I don't think there is a word invented yet that describes the way in which it makes you feel. You question yourself a bit after it.

During totality, you get a glimpse into the fact that there are forces and powers that we don't really know about. There is more going on than just our daily lives. There is a real connection with the planets, the Universe, people, and everything. Maybe it's energies we don't know about yet, or something deep down that we don't know how to use.

For me it was just magical—something unique I can't explain. You can imagine people in history before they understood the science of these things. What must they have felt? They would have just had these feelings deep inside them, with little understanding of what it was all about. They must have thought it was the end of the world.

Totality made me think of how quickly life goes. This is an event that everyone is building up for, and, within a minute or two, it's over. Gone. And life goes by like that as well. A lot of the worries we get are just insignificant; they mean nothing in the bigger picture. But we worry about them. Before you know it, life is gone and that is it. You have to grab life while you can. Nothing really matters.

I lost my mom when I was young—maybe this is why the eclipse affected me so much. I did think about my mom during totality because there was something greater and bigger going on. It brought me closer to my mom. I felt this link with nature, and I also felt a link with my mom. Everything was together. My mom is not physically here, but I know she is within me, and I know nature is within me. Totality was connecting me to everything. The whole thing—the bigger picture. When this happens, it makes you believe anything could happen.

How do we know what's next for us? When you are looking at how beautiful life is and how it is possible for totality to occur, how the hell do we guess what's coming next?

Something inside me changed, definitely, without a shadow of a doubt. I have been traveling around, partying, for a few years now. I felt like the total eclipse was a switch for me for a much healthier and wholesome way of life. I want to make a few lifestyle changes. It isn't just to do with the eclipse, but it's to do with the way I was feeling before. The eclipse helped me realize that there are shifts and changes. Seeing the total eclipse makes me want to stay healthy and live a nice life so I can experience amazing things in life.

I was in complete awe. Some hallucinogenic drugs can give you awe-inspiring experiences too, making you feel at one with everything. But at the end of the day, it's still a drug—you ingest something to experience it, but there can be an unwanted edge. Totality is a bit of a trip, to be sure; but it's like the most natural wholesome trip you are ever going to get. You don't need to take anything— it just happens. It's just a person and the world. There was no negativity, it is a natural high, pleasant and gentle and beautiful. After totality, I'm going to be a lot pickier about whether I indulge in these artificial things.

I believe seeing the total eclipse is good for you, and the more people who see it, the better. I saw the total eclipse in 1999, the year I started my period of partying. And now I've come here and have seen this eclipse, and this is the end of my reckless partying. There is a circle going on with the eclipse, and this is the end.

There is an old saying that lots of people walk through the meadow but only a few see the flowers within. I love that because that is so true. I think that would be the same with the eclipse: some people connect with it more than others.

Nothing is as amazing, beautiful, and inspirational as nature. When you are humbled by nature—whether it be the eclipse or swimming on the reef—you realize a few things. You don't need things like alcohol, money, and material things—you don't need them at all. The real happiness and real beauty is there for everyone. It's in us. I think the eclipse makes you realize the really special things don't cost money. It's about being. That's what it's all about.

I was meant to be here for this eclipse. I know I will see another one; it's just a matter of not *if* but *when*. Right now, I'm a bit hard up, so I can't really plan just yet. Life is short, and I just want to see as much as possible. I've done loads of cool stuff, and this has just topped it off. I will remember this experience of totality until my dying day. It will stay within me forever.

V. TERRY

The Festival-Goer

THE TOTAL ECLIPSE WAS REALLY great. I enjoyed it! It wasn't like a life-changing thing, and I wasn't freaked out. I didn't think the world was going to end. It was just pretty cool; it was good to see.

I was there at the festival in party mode, and I had a good time. I had some pretty intense experiences—not just with the total eclipse, but getting into the music, the trance state, and the dance.

I don't know how the eclipse would have been had I not taken anything. But substances give you this altered state of consciousness. I'm assuming that during the total eclipse, things can normally seem a bit harsh or strange. Substances added a nicer edge to it. It put me in a happy and cozy sort of place inside my own mind, as opposed to a weird one. It was stress-free—a bit more of a happy vibe. I suppose it sort of accentuated the emotions that I felt, sort of made them a bit more intense, and made me a bit more aware of what was happening. It just added an extra edge to the experience. It amplified things. It was good.

There are a lot of different people out there. The Eclipse Festival certainly showed me that. No matter how different we are in our everyday lives, there is something that appeals to every single person. For example, many people go out of their way to see the Queen when she visits Australia. Many would just go because it's a once-in-a-lifetime chance to see her in person. But it's not really for everyone—it's a personal taste thing.

But something like cosmic alignment—it's of broader appeal. So many different people were interested in the eclipse, across all age groups. We all shared this one experience. Of course, not every single person in the world would be into it; there will always be that margin that are simply not interested, for whatever reason. My friend who got too drunk and didn't wake up to the alarm—that's his loss. But a much larger percentage of people thought it was pretty good.

We are all part of nature and the Universe. It's not like humans going around on a speck of dust in the Universe.

We are all part of something bigger. We are all here for a reason. We are all from the same sort of creation.

VI. ROSE

The Wishful Teacher

I EXPECTED THE TOTAL ECLIPSE to be pretty interesting, and something that we would be lucky to be able to see. But I didn't expect it to be that good! I didn't want it to end. I felt that primitive fear, even though I knew what was going to happen. I think it's an instinctual response, what we feel at the time.

The funny thing is that I now get goosebumps whenever I talk or think about totality. I suppose it's the memory of it—what it feels like. It's like when people say, "Where were you when you heard the news about Lady Diana?" or something like that. It's one of those moments you will remember for life—where you were, what you were doing, and what you felt.

It probably sounds a bit strange, but I compare the totality experience to having my baby, in the way that it was life-changing. It was one of those life moments that was so big.

My colleague didn't see totality because of the clouds. He said it was good, but he can't relate to it being amazing. He said he understands the science of it, and therefore wouldn't get any emotional feelings even if he had seen it. But that is rubbish. I think it's because he doesn't know what he missed. That's my perception. You just have to experience it to know how untrue that belief is. If I hadn't seen it because of the clouds, I wouldn't have known what I had missed and how special it was.

We had one teacher at work who didn't get up to see the eclipse. She had no interest. What a loss for her. I just don't think you can get it unless you experience it yourself.

I have watched the recording of the live breakfast TV program a couple of times because it's nice to relive it. Seeing the presenters get overwhelmed was amazing. Every week, they are covering something special in a different part of Australia—they are used to seeing special things. You think they would become a bit desensitized to exciting things if they see them every week. But they were just as stunned as we were. It's powerful for people like me who are unable to travel. But it's never going to be the same, of course, as seeing it on TV.

I can't understand why the total eclipse is not advertised as *the* number-one thing to see in your life. I have read about the wonders of the world and the natural things you can travel to and experience. But I have never seen a total eclipse on those lists before. I don't know whether that is because of the precise time needed in a changeable, but specific location. It definitely deserves to be more well-known. It is one of the top life experiences. I don't understand why people don't travel to see it. Oh, sorry—there are people who travel to see it! But why don't we all know more about it?

Totality was nearly two minutes long where we were, and it felt like it took a long time. I completely forgot about everything else and was caught up in the moment.

I have an exhausting job and feel very busy. I'm probably not unusual in that. There are a million things on my mind and there is always something I need to be doing or should be doing. That's why the eclipse was special. It's not often that you take time to stop and look at where you are, and to focus on only one thing. During totality, I did not once think of anything else I had to do that day. I don't know if other people felt this way, but I couldn't think about anything else. I was just in that moment. I think that was one big thing I took out of the eclipse. I need to stop, pause, and reflect more. It is necessary to do that sometimes.

I have always been a bit curious about science. But I never before would have made a point of deliberately going out at night to see the stars or other astronomical events. The total eclipse experience has now made me interested in astronomy. I was out until a quarter past ten last night, and the Moon was quite beautiful. I'm now interested in seeing the phases of the Moon and what is in the sky at night time. I don't have a telescope—that is the first thing I need to work out. I've never thought about getting a telescope before.

The total eclipse has also captured my son's imagination. I want to encourage him to learn about the world as much as he can, while he is so amazed by it. We were down the esplanade last week, and we could see the Moon over here and the Sun over there. He jumped up and down and said, "Look, Mom, last time we saw them, they were together, and now they are so far apart." Wow, exactly! I hadn't even thought of it before. So that is all new territory that I am learning about and am trying to work out. The whole Universe.

The eclipse made me realize that we are little in the scheme of things. I'm a small part of it. That's how I feel when I travel—that nothing can go too wrong because I'm so little and the whole place is so big. But totality was so much bigger than what I personally experienced. It was about the whole Universe and the whole solar system. It is the biggest thing we can experience from Earth, short of space travel. I am amazed by the incredible coincidence—how everything lines up in those particular proportions, and that it even happens at all. It is all so very precise.

The total eclipse made me understand that we are here for such a short time. The Universe and planets have been around for such a long time. Our lifetime is so short—so much shorter on that scale than the two minutes of totality we experienced. We are only here for the blink of an eye. That is what I felt during totality.

It's a cliché, but you don't lie on your deathbed thinking, "I wish I had spent more time with my work colleagues, or working more, or spending more money." I imagine you would say, "I wish I had followed that passion." So if you are in a position to do what you can do to follow your passion, then that's fantastic. Hopefully down the road I will be.

I suppose it has made me think about my life circumstances and the practicalities. I'm limited in what I can do currently. I accept that and wouldn't have it any other way, but there is a frustration there. By keeping myself fit, active, and healthy, I will be able to go and see another total eclipse in the future. I suppose that is within my control.

But I suppose we are very lucky to be alive at this moment in time, to experience the total eclipse in this region. We were all there together on my mom's balcony, with a cup of coffee. So many things lined up that allowed me to see it in that special place, on that day, at that time, with my family. That moment will never happen again.

Now, some weeks after, everyone seems to be back in their normal daily lives. Yet I don't feel normal after totality. I feel I am the only one who is still affected! I can't understand why others don't feel this way. I don't know how long this excited feeling and inspiration will last. Life will continue, and the eclipse will become more distant. I don't know whether that effect will still be there in the future.

But I think it probably will.

4

LOOKING BACK
AT THE SHADOW

CHAPTER 7

WHAT CAN WE LEARN?

After reading the stories of our beings in the shadow, what lessons can we learn about the total solar eclipse experience?

I. It is a really big deal—and worth the hype

THE TOTAL SOLAR ECLIPSE REALLY is a big deal. If you haven't seen one, it can be hard to understand how epic the experience is. You can have the information about what to expect and how it happens, but nothing prepares you for how it *feels*. Totality is immersive—there are changes above you, around you, and within you.

Our beings in the shadow in the previous chapters were all surprised at how amazing it was. Cara could not see how a celestial event like an eclipse could trigger awe. Not only was she completely awestruck, but she also was overwhelmed and shaken by the experience, being reminded of how unexpected nature can be.

Peter had seen images of totality and had even observed a partial eclipse. Like Cara, he had no understanding of the intensity of totality, and was not planning to get into the path of totality. He was significantly impacted, and is now determined to chase eclipses along with storms.

Tabitha had been looking forward to the total eclipse for most of her adult life. Even *she* did not really know what was to happen, and the eclipse exceeded all of her expectations. Simon had experienced the darkness of totality before, but under cloud. Even he felt overwhelmed by this cloud-free totality experience. Terry had few expectations, and thought it was a great experience.

The thing that puzzled Rose the most: why the total solar eclipse was not more widely advertised as the number-one nature event to see in your life.

I've surveyed and interviewed hundreds of people after their eclipse experiences, and all are moved in some way. Some have said the experience was the catalyst for major changes in their lives. It changed my life. It could change yours.

II. The experience is difficult to communicate to others

IT IS DIFFICULT—IMPOSSIBLE, ALMOST—TO CONVEY to others how unique and incredible totality is. It is easy to see how doing a skydive could be exciting and thrilling, but most people do not see how an eclipse can be exciting and thrilling. Totality is an incredible experience. We feel an emotional rollercoaster of intense feelings within a short period. Most people shout out or scream the moment totality arrives. This joy can be heard in video clips of totality. Then there are the moments of introspection when people are in complete awe. What people feel in those moments is difficult to express. My surveys with eclipse chasers have identified commonalities in experience—the sense of wrongness, unsettled fear, awe, connectedness, euphoria, and desire to repeat the experience. These are outlined in detail in my first book *Total Addiction: The Life of an Eclipse Chaser*. The totality experience elicits an unsettled fear response that is difficult to explain, some calling it *primitive*. Simon described that deep feeling where we know something big was happening. Cara felt it too, and likened it to a feeling of unease that the natural order of things no longer can be trusted. Peter theorized that during all nature experiences, and especially totality, we tap into parts of our brain we don't normally access.

During a total eclipse, animals alter their behavior to changes in light. We too react to the changes in our environment.

III. Personal stories are needed for people to relate

NOT EVERYONE RELATES TO SCIENTISTS standing next to a telescope talking about the facts and figures of a total eclipse. Nor will they know what an animated video showing graphics of the Moon's shadow means for them personally. We need personal stories to highlight why something is relevant.

I have interviewed many people living within the path of totality before a total eclipse. The majority, including some in this book, do not relate to the total eclipse as a human experience until they hear someone talk about it with passion and excitement. Only then are they open to the possibility of thinking it will be of interest to them. Those living within the path are lucky, as they don't need to decide to travel to see the eclipse. They are also more likely to be exposed to eclipse outreach activities and able to hear personal stories. People living outside of the path need to seek information out and take action to get into the path of totality. This is one of my main motivations for writing this book: to help people learn that they should make the effort to get into the path of totality.

Of course, there will always be a small minority of people who are closed to the idea that the total eclipse is something unique and special. The most common rationale is that they understand the science, so they won't have an emotional response. Or else they say that they have seen totality before and it wasn't a big deal. Usually, they are incorrect on both counts. That will be their loss. But most people, given the chance, will want to experience something new. They find that the total eclipse experience exceeds all expectations. No one ever regrets seeing a total solar eclipse, but you will regret it if you miss an opportunity.

IV. The experience gives a feeling of connection

It is common to feel a connection to others who share the same experience, such as everyone who attends a musical event or sports game. The feeling of connection during totality is something bigger. You feel part of something greater, a feeling of peace and being at one with the world.

Our beings in the shadow made reference to feelings of connecting to our primitive ancestors. It's like you can relate to how people in the past would have felt, standing there as you are doing, bearing witness to totality. Our ancestors would have had similar feelings and emotions, without the benefit of our scientific understanding. This is a very common comment in all the interviews I have completed. Most feel insignificant yet an important part in the bigger picture. This is a comforting and empowering feeling.

The experience is a humbling reminder that we are all one as humans on this planet in this vast Universe. An experience that can unite people in such a powerful way—regardless of culture, background, color, political beliefs, gender, or sexual orientation—can only be a good thing. The world would be a better place if everyone could see a total solar eclipse.

V. You will want to repeat it

BEFORE THE ECLIPSE, YOU ARE likely to think that we eclipse chasers are a little weird, chasing astronomical events around the world. After experiencing totality, you will strongly identify with us. You will then most likely think we are the coolest people on the planet having figured all this out. We welcome you into the community of eclipse chasers!

Most of our beings in the shadow expressed a desire to see another total solar eclipse. They talked about the conflict between wanting to see one, yet not having resources to do so. Not everyone becomes an eclipse chaser. The difference between people who want to see one again and an eclipse chaser is that an eclipse chaser will make it happen. It will take absolute priority—we will always find a way. If the drive and desire is there, sacrifices will occur to make it happen. You can read more about what drives eclipse chasers in my first book, *Total Addiction: The Life of an Eclipse Chaser.*

VI. Weather is important

OUR BEINGS IN THE SHADOW were lucky to see and experience the total solar eclipse. Many others in the region, located along the coast, were clouded out. Totality will still occur, the Moon's shadow will still create a deep darkness, but clouds blocking the view will greatly reduce the experience. You do not see or experience the special features of totality, including seeing the eclipsed Sun, the corona, diamond rings, darkness of the sky, or seeing stars and planets during the day. Nor will you be able to experience the feeling of eeriness as the Moon's shadow creeps toward you.

Eclipse chasers will always prioritize clearer weather over length of time in totality. Make sure you position yourself in a way that maximizes your chances of seeing it. If your location is going to be cloudy, then consider moving to a location that has clearer skies. Be aware that traffic may impact your ability to move at the last moment. Deciding to move at the last moment is incredibly stressful—I did this myself in 2012 when I knew the clouds were not shifting. You can read stories about the differences in accounts between clear and cloudy skies from 2012 in my second book, *Totality: The Total Solar Eclipse of 2012 in Far North Queensland.*

VII. You need to know about eye safety

LOOKING AT THE SUN WITHOUT protecting your eyes can cause permanent damage, during an eclipse or not. The only way to safely view the Sun is to use approved solar filters, often manufactured as eclipse glasses. These are cheap and should be purchased early, as they are often limited in supply. They are a safety device and should be treated carefully to avoid getting scratched or damaged.

Using them is simple. Put them on, and then look up toward the Sun. It is exciting to see the Sun for the first time using solar filters, as it seems bigger than what we imagine.

Outside of the path of totality, solar filters are needed to view the partial eclipse at all times. Within the path of totality, solar filters are needed during the partial phases. However, the few minutes of totality can be viewed directly with the naked eye. This is because the Sun is not visible, so you are not damaging your eyes. You will see the corona of the Sun, which emits a wispy, ethereal light. It is a stunning sight and safe to view. Most of our beings in the shadow knew intuitively when their filters could be removed.

The American Astronomical Society and NASA provide official eye safety advice, based upon extensive research and experience. This guidance is reprinted in Section 5. Astronomers, solar researchers, and of course eclipse chasers have been safely using filters to view eclipses for many decades.

Before every eclipse, there is usually some group or expert giving dated and misinformed guidance on eye safety. Their motivation is not to encourage or inform people. Instead, their aim is to protect themselves from any potential litigation. They may state the following:

- *There is no way to safely view totality (wrong)*
- *Approved solar filters are not safe to view the Sun (wrong)*
- *The best way to see a total eclipse is to watch it on TV (wrong)*
- *You should turn your back during totality (wrong)*

These suggestions are seriously outdated. But crucially, incorrect guidance can create confusion, with potentially devastating consequences. Be clear and confident about how to safely view the eclipse, and always refer to the official safety guidance. Any information that contradicts this reliable guidance is wrong.

Cara's partner Mike, who had a mini-freakout, raises a few important issues. His experience shows that even levelheaded, intelligent people can still be affected by the total eclipse. Mike had heard the general repeated warnings not to look at the eclipse. He also heard the misinformation given a few days prior to the eclipse, stating all of the incorrect facts above. Mike had not looked in detail at the official eye safety guidance, whereas Cara had. They had no idea they had different understandings of safe viewing until it played out during those precious moments of totality.

Mike had two different but conflicting responses to totality. First, he felt it was so otherworldly that he didn't trust what he knew—surely it's not safe?

> *I hadn't done much research about it. All I kept hearing was, "Don't look at it—you will burn your eyes." But that was only the partial. When totality happened, I tried the glasses and I couldn't see anything at all. I then looked directly at the eclipsed Sun, but it looked so wrong. I thought you could look, but then seeing it, I figured I must have misunderstood—surely you can't look at that!*

Second, he felt it was *so* otherworldly that he couldn't *not* look! Even when he thought that he *shouldn't* look, he found himself peering through his fingers. He couldn't help himself. As a result of these two conflicts, Mike lost precious totality time that he can never get back.

Tabitha also felt that urge to look for as long as possible, and was prompted several times to put her glasses back on:

> *I didn't put my glasses on straight away because I wanted to keep watching it. At the time, I did think I had done something to my eyes. To be honest, I was like, "Oh well, whatever." By the end of it, I saw little circles, I felt sort of drunk on the eclipse. For a while, I was a little worried about my eyes.*

She felt the sacrifice of looking was worth any potential damage to her eyes. This is not a view to be encouraged, but we need to be aware that this happens. Tabitha's symptoms remained for a short period, but she could have caused long-term damage.

I have interviewed several people who took advice literally and kept their solar filters on even during totality—despite not being able to see anything. They did not look around to see the changes in light. They felt very disappointed afterward when they realized they missed it all. The best thing to do is to use your eclipse glasses periodically to check the progress of the partial phases. Don't keep your filters on the whole time. Keep looking around you to observe the many changes in your environment.

Totality can be so overwhelming that many people are thrown by it. It looks wrong, and it is easy to doubt what you think you know. This is why any confusion over eye safety may increase risk of damage. Always refer to the official guidance, and understand it before the eclipse. Bring the official safe-viewing guidance with you. If you are not confident about eye safety, then go to an event where there is someone guiding on when it is safe to view.

CHAPTER 8

CONCLUSION:
GET INTO THE PATH

If you live within the path of totality, you must understand how lucky you are. Not only will you experience a total solar eclipse, but you will also experience it from within your region. This occurs on average once every 375 years. Most eclipse chasers have to travel around the world to get to where you live. We also have to be on the roads in the traffic and find places to stay. Whereas you just have to roll out of bed—how lucky you are! You can always chase another eclipse, but you can *never* get back the experience of seeing it within your own community.

Our beings in the shadow recognized that they would not have experienced the total eclipse if they had not lived within or near the path of totality. If you happen to live within a path of totality, do all you can to let others know to get into the path. Lack of information is the main barrier; people will find out eventually, and often then, it is too late.

If you live outside of the path of totality, do all you can to get into the path. This point cannot be stressed enough: to experience the full wonder of the total solar eclipse, you must get into the path of totality. Even a 99 percent partial eclipse does not offer the full experience of the total eclipse. You will miss the main show. Do not let anyone tell you that staying outside of the path is the best option. It is not. Friends don't let friends miss out.

It really is a coincidence that the total eclipse can happen at all. But the total eclipse is not just an astronomical event. It is a human event and of interest to everyone, not just geeks, scientists, and eclipse chasers. Our beings in the shadow had their own unique experiences and made sense of totality in their own way. Yet you will have noted some common threads throughout their eclipse experience. All described how it was difficult to put into words. All stressed that it was a unique event that had to be experienced to be understood. All experienced unexpected, intense, emotional reactions during totality. And all felt their worldview had changed following the experience, with some wanting to become eclipse chasers.

I hope by reading the stories of these ordinary people that you are now excited and curious to see a total solar eclipse. Perhaps you want to try a molten chocolate lava cake too. Life is all about the experiences we have and the people we share them with. With totality, it is all about being in the shadow.

*"When it comes time to die,
let us not discover that we have never lived."*

—*Henry David Thoreau*

5

ADDITIONAL INFORMATION

Official Eye Safety Guidance (AAS)

Looking directly at the Sun is unsafe except during the brief total phase of a solar eclipse ("totality"), when the Moon entirely blocks the Sun's bright face, which will happen only within the narrow path of totality (http://bit.ly/1xuYxSu).

The only safe way to look directly at the uneclipsed or partially eclipsed Sun is through special-purpose solar filters, such as "eclipse glasses" or hand-held solar viewers. Homemade filters or ordinary sunglasses, even very dark ones, are not safe for looking at the Sun. To date four manufacturers have certified that their eclipse glasses and hand-held solar viewers meet the ISO 12312-2 international standard for such products: Rainbow Symphony, American Paper Optics, Thousand Oaks Optical, and TSE 17.

- Always inspect your solar filter before use; if scratched or damaged, discard it. Read and follow any instructions printed on or packaged with the filter. Always supervise children using solar filters.

- Stand still and cover your eyes with your eclipse glasses or solar viewer before looking up at the bright Sun. After glancing at the Sun, turn away and remove your filter — do not remove it while looking at the Sun.

- Do not look at the uneclipsed or partially eclipsed Sun through an unfiltered camera, telescope, binoculars, or other optical device. Similarly, do not look at the Sun through a camera, a telescope, binoculars, or any other optical device while using your eclipse glasses or hand-held solar viewer — the concentrated solar rays will damage the filter and enter your eye(s), causing serious injury. Seek expert advice from an astronomer before using a solar filter with a camera, a telescope, binoculars, or any other optical device.

- If you are within the path of totality (http://bit. ly/1xuYxSu), remove your solar filter only when the Moon completely covers the Sun's bright face and it suddenly gets quite dark. Experience totality, then, as soon as the bright Sun begins to reappear, replace your solar viewer to glance at the remaining partial phases. An alternative method for safe viewing of the partially eclipsed Sun is pinhole projection. For example, cross the outstretched, slightly open fingers of one hand over the outstretched, slightly open fingers of the other. With your back to the Sun, look at your hands' shadow on the ground. The little spaces between your fingers will project a grid of small images on the ground, showing the Sun as a crescent during the partial phases of the eclipse. A solar eclipse is one of nature's grandest spectacles. By following these simple rules, you can safely enjoy the view and be rewarded with memories to last a lifetime. More information: eclipse.aas.org eclipse2017.nasa.gov

Content and image reprinted with permission from the American Astronomical Society. A PDF version can be downloaded from https://eclipse.aas.org/eye-safety/safe-viewing.

List of Total Eclipses until 2030

The most popular question after people see their first total solar eclipse is this: when is the next one?

This list of the total solar eclipses occurring in the next decade or so will come in handy. The countries listed are a guide only—make sure to fully explore the path of totality for each map.

All maps of the path for the eclipses below can be found on the website of Xavier Jubier, a French eclipse chaser: http://xjubier.free.fr/en/site_pages/SolarEclipsesGoogleMaps.html

Be warned that exploring eclipse maps is addictive and time-consuming!

- August 21, 2017 in the United States of America

- July 2, 2019 in Chile or Argentina

- December 14, 2020 in Chile or Argentina

- December 4, 2021 in Antarctica

- April 20, 2023 in Australia or Indonesia (hybrid)

- April 8, 2024 in Mexico, USA, Canada

- August 12, 2026 in Spain, Iceland, Greenland

- August 2, 2027 in Spain, North Africa, Middle East

- July 22, 2028 in Australia, New Zealand

- November 25, 2030 in Africa, Australia

Previous Works

This book is my third published book about the total eclipse experience. Information about my other publications, including order information, can be seen on my website www.beingtheshadow.com.

Total Addiction:
The Life of an Eclipse Chaser, 2012

Experiencing a total eclipse is a life-changing event for many people and is described by some as an unforgettable event to experience at least once in your life. However, there are many people who believe that once in a lifetime is not enough. These people—eclipse chasers—travel every eighteen months or so to very specific locations around the world in order to experience a total solar eclipse.

In *Total Addiction: The Life of an Eclipse Chaser*, Dr. Russo explains how solar eclipses occur and describes the emotional reactions that many people have when they see a total eclipse. By analyzing the phenomenological interviews of nine eclipse chasers, Dr. Russo is able to describe the key human experiences of totality and how the experience impacts upon our sense of time, place, and person. Also explained is how eclipse chasers are able to sustain their motivation for their passion, often for decades.

Those who have seen a total eclipse will find this book useful in helping them to understand their often-overwhelming experience. Those not lucky enough to have seen a total solar eclipse will obtain a glimpse into the intriguing world of the eclipse chaser, and perhaps by the end of it, will want to experience totality for themselves.

Totality:
The Total Solar Eclipse of 2012
in Far North Queensland, 2013

This beautiful souvenir book features personal stories of people experiencing the eclipse, as well as stunning images, and is narrated by Dr. Kate Russo, an eclipse-chasing psychologist from Far North Queensland.

By combining stories and images, Dr. Russo has managed to bring to life this incredibly rare event in a way that allows readers to get an insider's perspective of the eclipse. From the clear outback to the cloudy coastline, from coral cay islands and even underwater, these accounts convey the personal impact of totality and what it was like to be there in Far North Queensland during totality.

The book also includes fantastic eclipse images taken within the region by award-winning eclipse photographers.

If you have seen a total solar eclipse, or you would like to experience one, then you will enjoy *Totality.* The book allows you to get an insight into the powerful experience of the eclipse, to understand why it is often described as a once-in-a-lifetime event. The book would be of particular appeal to those living in communities along the path of totality.

White Paper on
Community Eclipse Planning, 2015

The purpose of this document is to provide introductory guidance for the planning of the total solar eclipse within your community. It includes an overview of the complexities of planning for this once-in-a-lifetime event in your region. The three core messages are: start planning early; focus on the community in addition to eclipse tourists; and consult with eclipse experts to help with the unknowns.

The white paper can be downloaded directly from www. beingintheshadow.com.

Get Involved!

Before and after every total eclipse, I gather research material about the eclipse experience. If you would like to take part by completing surveys and interviews, then please follow me on social media to get the latest information and sign up for the newsletter.

I am continually adding to my website a collection of videos and stories about aspects of the total eclipse experience. Make sure to listen to my own video clips and clips from other eclipse chasers. If you would like to contribute, send your stories to research@beingintheshadow.com. Video clips can be sent to the same address using WeTransfer for larger files. Video clips should ideally be a minute long, and instructions will usually be given for specific projects.

All of my eclipse research is self-funded. Please support my projects by purchasing my books, requesting my books to be in your local library, and giving them as gifts to others who may not know about the eclipse experience. Donations are possible through my website. I am also open to sponsorship arrangements to allow me to continue my research projects and outreach activities.

You can also join me on tour. I lead eclipse tours with *The Independent Traveller*, and will be viewing the 2017 total eclipse from Teton Village, Wyoming. NOTE: *This tour is now sold out.*

Finally, you can join me at my many eclipse outreach events by keeping an eye on my upcoming events on my website and on social media. Consider bringing me in as a speaker if you feel sharing personal stories about the eclipse experience, and the psychology of the eclipse experience, is of interest to your audience. See my website for details.

Has this book changed the way you view the total eclipse? If so, then please consider leaving a review on Amazon.

Facebook: @Beingintheshadow

Twitter: @DrKateRusso

Website: www.beingintheshadow.com

Acknowledgments

I WOULD LIKE TO THANK the many people who have helped me bring this book to completion.

First, to the beings in the shadow—Cara, Peter, Tabitha, Simon, Terry, and Rose. These people are the heart and soul of this book. My wish is for you all to get into the path of totality for the second time.

To my sister, Vicki Russo, my main support for my research and writing projects. A long way away, yet always there when needed. Remember, 2028 is not long to wait.

To Terry Moseley, my eclipse mentor for many years now. For support, guidance, fact-checking, writing critique, and good craic and conversation. Thanks also to Paul Money for additional guidance when needed. Sincerest thanks also to Rick Fienberg. Your time, patience and support for this project, and beyond, has been much appreciated.

To my early reviewers—Gary Millar, David Moncrieff, Richard Scott, and Bambi Leigh Hale. Thanks for your time, and for not being scared to tell me when I'm going around in circles.

To Carol Graham, for painting an awesome cover based upon my (poor) descriptions and images of totality. I hope you get to be in the path one day too, and paint what inspires you.

To Shayla Eaton, for copyediting and proofing the book. I have learned so much through our short time together, and am a better writer for it.

To Melinda Martin, for interior and final cover layout. Thanks for supporting me through the many steps involved in publishing this book.

Finally, to my partner of twenty years, Geordie, who recently became my husband. Always by my side at every total eclipse, and through many recent life challenges. Long may you be an *eclipse chaser-chaser*.

About Dr. Kate Russo

DR. KATE RUSSO IS AN author, psychologist, and eclipse chaser.

With a professional background in psychology, Kate is a highly skilled eclipse-planning consultant. She is one of the very few eclipse chasers who has experienced a total solar eclipse in her own home region, and knows firsthand the challenges involved in preparing a community for the total eclipse. She was involved in eclipse events and outreach for 2012 in Australia, and was the eclipse-planning consultant for the Faroe Islands in 2015.

Drawing upon her consulting and academic skills, she then researched and wrote the White Paper on Community Eclipse Planning in late 2015—a document that has been used by hundreds of communities across the US in preparation for the August 2017 total eclipse. She has already helped many communities in the path in their approach to planning.

Along with her expertise in eclipse planning, Kate is the recognized authority on the total solar eclipse experience. She answers the key question: what is it like to experience a total solar eclipse? Not only is she able to talk from her personal experiences of seeing ten total solar eclipses, but she can also share the experiences of the hundreds of others she has surveyed and interviewed. She has authored three books on the topic, and is in demand as a speaker and in the media before every eclipse. She has been featured in several eclipse documentaries and books. She is a passionate speaker who can relate to a wide range of audiences.

Originally from Australia, Kate has lived in Belfast, Northern Ireland for the last twenty years with her Australian partner Geordie. She has had a successful career in clinical psychology specializing in health and illness. She also spent six years as assistant course director for a doctoral training program in clinical psychology at Queen's University Belfast. She developed expertise in a research methodology known as Interpretative Phenomenological Analysis, which she uses in her eclipse research. Kate still maintains an academic link and is research facilitator of IPA Australia; peer reviews academic research in IPA and undertakes private research consulting when she is not chasing eclipses.

Visit Kate's website at www.beingintheshadow.com and join her mailing list if you would like to be kept informed of her activities and research. She is most active on Facebook @beingintheshadow.

40930501R00081